Praise for *Teaching for Deeper Learning*

Jay McTighe and Harvey Silver bring together their wealth of knowledge and ideas around powerful thinking skills, essential questions, and concept-based curriculum to help teachers effect deep learning and transfer. They had the insight to see how using seven major thinking skills to facilitate greater knowledge acquisition could become the springboard to the crafting of "big ideas"— the transferable, conceptual understandings that reflect deep learning. This easy-to-read book flows from chapter to chapter with practical tools, ideas, and examples to guide the teacher in facilitating meaning making.

Education offers a plethora of individual innovations, but when curriculum and instruction leaders can combine the power of the best ideas to create not only a higher-order end but also a clear means to that end, then they have truly made a significant contribution to the field. This book is one of those contributions.

—Dr. H. Lynn Erickson, author and presenter

This is the book you'll want to extend your instructional skills and expand your backpack of strategies to support how the brain learns best. By engaging thinking skills to help students actively process information, teachers leverage the brain's executive functions to deepen student understanding and achieve learning that lasts.

I have room for only five reference books on my desk, and *Teaching for Deeper Learning* just took over the top spot.

—Judy Willis, MD, MEd,
Board-certified neurologist, teacher, author, and consultant

Because all the knowledge in the world is on the phone in nearly every student's pocket, a person's ability to thrive in the modern world is based on their ability to analyze the veracity of information, make sense of its context and perspective, draw conclusions, take responsible action (often in concert with others), assess the impact of that action, and reassess based on new information. *Teaching for Deeper Learning* gives teachers the tools to equip students with these critical capacities.

—Michael R. Cornell, Superintendent,
Hamburg Central School District (New York)

TEACHING FOR
DEEPER
LEARNING

ASCD MEMBER BOOK

Many ASCD members received this book as a
member benefit upon its initial release.

Learn more at: **www.ascd.org/memberbooks**

TEACHING FOR
DEEPER
LEARNING

Tools to Engage Students in
Meaning Making

JAY **MCTIGHE** | HARVEY F. **SILVER**

ascd

Arlington, Virginia USA

2800 Shirlington Road, Suite 1001 • Arlington, VA 22206 USA
Phone: 800-933-2723 or 703-578-9600 • Fax: 703-575-5400
Website: www.ascd.org • E-mail: member@ascd.org
Author guidelines: www.ascd.org/write

Ranjit Sidhu, *Executive Director and CEO;* Stefani Roth, *Publisher;* Genny Ostertag, *Director, Content Acquisitions;* Julie Houtz, *Director, Book Editing & Production;* Miriam Calderone, *Editor;* Judi Connelly, *Senior Art Director;* Melissa Johnston, *Graphic Designer;* Cynthia Stock, *Typesetter;* Kelly Marshall, *Interim Manager, Production Services;* Trinay Blake, *E-Publishing Specialist;* Tristan Coffelt, *Senior Production Specialist*

PAPERBACK ISBN: 978-1-4166-2862-0   ASCD product #120022
PDF E-BOOK ISBN: 978-1-4166-2864-4; see Books in Print for other formats.
Quantity discounts are available: e-mail programteam@ascd.org or call 800-933-2723, ext. 5773, or 703-575-5773. For desk copies, go to www.ascd.org/deskcopy.

ASCD Member Book No. FY20-4A (Jan. 2020 PSI+). ASCD Member Books mail to Premium (P), Select (S), and Institutional Plus (I+) members on this schedule: Jan, PSI+; Feb, P; Apr, PSI+; May, P; Jul, PSI+; Aug, P; Sep, PSI+; Nov, PSI+; Dec, P. For current details on membership, see www.ascd.org/membership.

Library of Congress Cataloging-in-Publication Data
Names: McTighe, Jay, author. | Silver, Harvey F., author.
Title: Teaching for deeper learning : tools to engage students in meaning making / Jay McTighe, Harvey F. Silver.
Description: Alexandria, VA : ASCD, 2020. | Includes bibliographical references and index. | Summary: "Jay McTighe and Harvey Silver offer a practical guide to teaching seven essential thinking skills that will equip students for success in school and beyond"—Provided by publisher.
Identifiers: LCCN 2019040170 (print) | LCCN 2019040171 (ebook) | ISBN 9781416628620 (paperback) | ISBN 9781416628644 (pdf)
Subjects: LCSH: Concept learning. | Critical thinking—Study and teaching. | Motivation in education.
Classification: LCC LB1062 .M388 2020 (print) | LCC LB1062 (ebook) | DDC 370.15/23--dc23
LC record available at https://lccn.loc.gov/2019040170
LC ebook record available at https://lccn.loc.gov/2019040171

30 29 28 27 26 25 24 23   5 6 7 8 9 10 11 12

Sir Isaac Newton said the reason he saw so far is that he stood on the shoulders of giants. We have also worked with two giants: Richard Strong and Grant Wiggins. They were wonderful friends, colleagues, and education thought leaders. Although they are no longer with us, their ideas are alive within this book, which we humbly dedicate to them.

———————————————

TEACHING FOR DEEPER LEARNING

Tools to Engage Students in **Meaning Making**

Acknowledgments

Writing this book was a labor of love for both of us. It's not a simple task to synthesize ideas from nearly 100 years of collective work developed over two parallel careers. Throughout the process, we have had rich conversations, raised questions, and even debated several points, but in the end, we think this text represents a truly collaborative integration of the ideas of Understanding by Design® and The Thoughtful Classroom™.

The publication of our book would not have been possible without the help of a marvelous writing team. We would like to thank Matthew Perini, a master craftsman and wordsmith whose guidance and direction were essential in helping us achieve a synthesis of our ideas; Abigail Boutz, a critical friend who helped ensure that our writing was clear and our tools and strategies were practical and user-friendly; Justin Gilbert, our internal editor who made sure that all the details were correct and that the manuscript was delivered on time; and Kimberly Nunez, whose willingness to jump in and help throughout the process saved us more than once.

We would also like to acknowledge ASCD for its support throughout the years and for giving us the opportunity to share our ideas with the field. In particular, we thank the ASCD publishing team, notably Stefani Roth, Genny Ostertag, and our capable editor, Miriam Calderone, for their support from the book's inception to its publication.

Finally, we give thanks to the thousands of teachers and administrators with whom we have worked during our long careers. We have learned so much from you, and we hope that our book will give something back to the profession.

—Jay and Harvey

Preface

Legend has it that the world-renowned architect and thinker Buckminster Fuller once told an aspiring young architect that a great design must achieve four goals. Fuller framed these goals as the following four simple questions:

1. Does the design meet its intended purpose?
2. Is it functional?
3. Will people like it?
4. Is it beautiful?

These four questions have guided the design of this book. First, we set out with a clear *purpose:* to help educators make the critical shift from providing information to students (a knowledge consumption model) to empowering students to become active meaning makers who seek deep understanding and are able to transfer their learning.

Second, because it has been our experience that educators are looking for resources that are practical and easy to implement in their classrooms, we strove to make our book highly *functional,* providing a wealth of ready-to-use tools and strategies to help you put its ideas into practice immediately.

To help us address the question *Will people like it?,* we have tested and refined the book's ideas and tools in our workshops, coaching partnerships, and professional development work in schools. We are proud to say that the feedback from educators has been extremely positive and enthusiastic.

Then there's that last question, the most subjective one of all: *Is it beautiful?* One way to think of beauty is as something that is both simple and deep, like a haiku—easy to comprehend but profound in its effect. In writing a book full of simple tools designed to create deep change in classrooms and schools, we sincerely hope that we have met this beautiful standard of simplicity and depth. Most important, we hope that we inspire you—a designer of instruction—to see the beauty in what you teach, in how you teach it, and in the impact your work has on students' futures.

Introduction

Mitosis versus *meiosis,* logarithms, the Battle of Hastings: can you recall a time in high school or college when you "learned" something and were able to pass a test on it, only to quickly forget it? Perhaps the information was not important to you, or maybe you only learned it by rote. Cognitive psychologists have characterized such learning as *inert* knowledge—learning that was superficially acquired, never really understood, and promptly forgotten (National Research Council, 2000). Now contrast those examples with something that you *really* understand—learning that has endured. What is the difference in how you came to learn and understand it? What can you now do because of that understanding?

These differences are familiar to us, and they underscore one of the chief goals of this book: to promote deep and lasting learning that enhances the retention of information, leads to conceptual understanding, and equips students to be able to transfer their learning to new situations.

But what does it mean to learn something deeply? We propose that deep learning results in enduring understanding of important ideas and processes. However, we also contend that understanding must be "earned" by the learner. In other words, understanding is not something that teachers can transmit simply by telling. Although we can directly teach facts and procedures, understanding of conceptually larger ideas and abstract processes must be constructed in the mind of the learner. Students earn understanding through the active mental manipulation of content via higher-order

1

thinking skills. We refer to this active construction of meaning by students as *meaning making*.

When deep learning and understanding are the goals, the teacher's role expands from that of primarily a dispenser of information or modeler of a skill (the sage on the stage) to a facilitator of meaning making (a guide on the side). More specifically, teachers facilitate understanding of classroom content by helping students process that content using thinking skills that engage them in active meaning making.

In this book, we highlight the following seven thinking skills:

1. Conceptualizing
2. Note making and summarizing
3. Comparing
4. Reading for understanding
5. Predicting and hypothesizing
6. Visualizing and graphic representation
7. Perspective taking and empathizing

Use of these seven skills helps students achieve deep and lasting learning by facilitating acquisition of information for greater retention and retrieval, fostering active meaning making that leads to deeper understanding of "big ideas," and building the ability to apply, or transfer, learning to new situations both within school and beyond.

Why *These* Skills?

Obviously, there are a great many thinking skills that can enhance meaning making and understanding. So why did we select these seven in particular? We have made these skills the focus of this book for the following reasons:

- *They embody the essentials of good thinking.* Good thinkers employ these skills in school, at work, and in life. They are deeply embedded in current academic standards and standardized tests. What's more, they are the foundations of more complex forms of reasoning, such as argument, inquiry, and design.

- *They separate high achievers from their average- or low-performing peers.* Through our many years of research and work in schools, we have found that successful students are able to handle the cognitive demands of complex work and rigorous content precisely because they enlist these skills to help them. Students who struggle with complexity and learning challenges tend to lack many of these thinking skills.

- *They are often undertaught.* Considering how vital these skills are to students' learning and academic success, it is striking how rarely they are directly taught in our classrooms. In fact, these skills are sometimes so hard to find that we might call them the "hidden skills of academic success." But if we are to hold ourselves responsible for preparing our students to meet the demands of rigorous cognitive and content challenges, then we must help them become better able to respond to such challenges. Teaching and reinforcing these seven skills are how such "response-ability" develops and how college and career readiness is realized.

- *They give all teachers a manageable way to raise achievement and increase student success.* We intentionally selected skills that cut across content areas and grade levels. No matter your grade or subject specialty, you can teach, assess, and benchmark these skills with relative ease. Plus, seven is a manageable number of skills to master—and we know from experience just how crucial manageability is to successful classroom implementation.

In sum, the thinking skills and tools that we've chosen to focus on have a dual benefit: (1) as a *means,* they support active construction of meaning by students, leading to deeper understanding of core content; and (2) as an *end,* they provide inherently valuable, transferable skills and tools that students can use throughout school and life. The tools, therefore, are as much for students as they are for you.

How the Book Is Organized

While our primary goal in putting this book together was to provide educators with concrete skills and tools for engaging students in active meaning making and deep learning, we felt that the book wouldn't be complete without also discussing what kind of content is worth making meaning about, how to incorporate the featured skills and tools into lesson and unit design, and how to build students' capacity to use the tools independently. Thus, we've made sure to address each of these important elements within the book's nine chapters. Let's look at how the information is organized.

Chapter 1 discusses what's worth having students understand and make meaning about. It emphasizes the importance of establishing a conceptually based curriculum to ensure that teaching and learning stay focused on important and transferable ideas, and it presents practical tools and strategies for doing so.

Chapters 2–8 explore the seven meaning-making skills in depth. The "how" section of each chapter is where you'll find practical and proven tools and strategies for targeting the skill in the classroom, along with illustrative examples that can help you use the tools and strategies more effectively.

Chapter 9 provides specific ideas to help you incorporate the book's strategies into your repertoire, as well as your students'. It presents a tried-and-true instructional process for teaching students to use the tools independently, illustrates how to infuse the skills and tools within curriculum units to engage students in active meaning making, and shows how you can use a curriculum Mapping Matrix to map out the units over an entire year to ensure that you are focusing on big ideas and systematically employing thinking skills to help students understand these ideas.

Tools Make It Possible

Just as humans throughout history have used tools like the wheel, the astrolabe, the mechanical plow, and the computer to make their work easier and more effective, you can use the tools in this book to enhance *your* work as an educator. Instead of abstract, hard-to-implement ideas, these tools provide concrete and simple ways to promote deep and active learning, a means of making abstract and internal thinking processes visible, and a vehicle for bringing principles of sound instruction into your classroom in a format that both you and your students will enjoy.

1

Framing Learning Around Big Ideas

In the Introduction, we discussed the importance of actively engaging students in meaning making. In Chapters 2–8, we'll explore thinking skills and tools that can help students make meaning of the content we teach. But what should we be teaching in the first place? What's worth having students understand and make meaning about? How can we design our curriculum in a way that promotes deep learning and transfer?

To address these questions, we need to consider several factors that affect a modern-day education. A fundamental characteristic of our world is the fact that our collective knowledge base continues to increase rapidly, with estimated doubling times that are expressed in months rather than decades. Indeed, knowledge is expanding faster than we're able to absorb it. And the accompanying reality that ordinary people can now access much of that knowledge on a smartphone means that contemporary schooling no longer requires memorization of all pertinent information.

A related trend has to do with the rapidity, and related unpredictability, of changes in today's world. From technological advances (e.g., automation and artificial intelligence) to political and economic transformations, shifts in global migration patterns, and climatic change, it is fair to say that we are no longer educating learners for a stable and predictable world.

Focus on Big Ideas

Clearly, our world is changing dramatically—and the focus of our teaching needs to change in response. Attentiveness to trends like the ones described above has driven leading curriculum experts (Erickson, 2007, 2008; Wiggins & McTighe, 2005, 2011, 2012) to recommend that a modern curriculum be prioritized around a smaller number of conceptually larger, transferable ideas. They make this recommendation for four reasons:

1. *There is simply too much information to be able to cover it all in school.* The explosion of knowledge means that we can address only a relatively small amount of all possible content, especially in history and the STEM subjects (science, technology, engineering, and math). This makes it imperative to identify the big ideas that are essential for students to understand and to focus instruction accordingly.

2. *Trying to cover too much content can result in superficial and disengaged learning.* By contrast, when we focus on fewer but bigger ideas and transferable skills, we have more time to engage students actively in making meaning of those big ideas. Moreover, we can expand the use of performance tasks that involve students in applying their learning in authentic and meaningful ways, leading to deeper learning and transfer abilities.

3. *An emphasis on larger ideas reflects our understanding of how knowledge is best structured for retention and use.* Research on how experts' knowledge is organized relative to that of novices reveals that "[experts'] knowledge is not simply a list of facts and formulas that are relevant to their domain; instead, their knowledge is organized around core concepts or 'big ideas' that guide their thinking about their domains" (National Research Council, 2000, p. 36).

4. *The rapid changes and unpredictability of the modern world call for learners who will be able to* transfer *their learning.* Rote learning of factual information will not, by itself, equip learners to effectively apply it to new situations. Because transfer requires an understanding of broader concepts and generalizations, teaching for transfer requires focusing on conceptually bigger ideas.

Please note that our recommended emphasis on big ideas and transferable processes is not meant to minimize the importance of teaching basic skills or foundational knowledge. We simply propose that basic facts and skills should be treated as a means to greater ends—in other words, as raw material for developing the larger conceptual understandings that we want students to walk away with. It is noteworthy that the most recent generation of standards in the United States—including the Common Core State Standards, the Next Generation Science Standards, and the College, Career, and Civic Life (C3) Framework for Social Studies—all emphasize teaching for deep understanding of larger concepts rather than superficially covering vast amounts of information.

Concept-Based Curriculum Design

The sheer volume of potential content and the corresponding problem of "mile-wide, inch-deep" curriculum require curriculum teams and individual teachers to be able to prioritize—that is, to determine the most important curricular outcomes, as well as the best use of available instructional time. By focusing curriculum around conceptually important and transferable ideas, teachers can go into greater depth to develop and deepen students' understanding rather than simply trying to cover large volumes of discrete facts.

In this chapter, we describe three approaches that teachers can use to frame curriculum and instruction around important ideas:

1. **A Study In . . .** encourages teachers to plan their units to focus on the key concepts to be understood rather than just topics, skills, or texts.

2. **Concept Word Wall** reminds teachers to identify the key concepts that will help students develop a deep understanding of the content—and to make those concepts visible in the classroom.

3. **Essential Questions** shows teachers how to frame their content around open-ended and thought-provoking questions that help students make meaning of and "uncover" the big ideas.

A Study In . . .

A simple yet effective way to ensure that an instructional unit maintains a conceptual focus rather than just addressing topics, basic skills, or activities is to frame it as "a study in" a larger, transferable concept or theme (Silver & Perini, 2010). Select an appropriate concept or theme (see Figure 1.1 for a list of possibilities), build it into your unit title, and use the selected concept to focus instruction over the course of the unit. Here are some examples of units that were framed in this manner:

- Argument Writing: A Study in *Craftsmanship*
- Impressionism: A Study in *Revolution*
- The Four Seasons: A Study in *Change*
- The Pentagon Papers: A Study in *Deception*
- Four Films by Hitchcock: A Study in *Obsession*
- Weight Training: A Study in *Proper Technique*
- Whole Numbers: A Study in *Rules and Relationships*
- Formal Versus Informal Forms of Address in Spanish: A Study in *Respect*

When deciding which concept to pick for a given unit, remember that there's no "correct" choice; the choice should be supportive of targeted standards and reflect whatever big idea or message you want to highlight. A team of English language arts (ELA) teachers, for example, considered framing a unit on argument writing as a study in *perspective,* a study in *balance,* or a study in *persuasion*—but ultimately decided on a study in *craftsmanship* because they wanted to emphasize the idea that crafting an argument takes care and skill. An art history teacher similarly considered different ways to frame a unit on Impressionism but went with "Impressionism: A Study in *Revolution"* because he felt that *revolution* best captured the central idea that he wanted students to understand and remember: that the Impressionists "overthrew" the established mode of painting and replaced it with one that was radically different in terms of both style and subject matter.

Note that the idea of framing learning around larger concepts and themes shouldn't be limited to teachers. In the next chapter, we'll show you

FIGURE 1.1

Examples of Transferable Concepts and Themes

abundance/scarcity	design	mood
acceptance/rejection	discovery	movement
adaptation	diversity	needs and wants
balance	environment	order
caring	equality/inequality	organization
cause and effect	equilibrium	parts and wholes
challenge	equivalence	patriotism
change/continuity	ethics	patterns
character	evolution	perseverance
communication	exploitation	perspective
community	exploration	prejudice
competition	fairness	production/consumption
composition	freedom	relationships
conflict	friendship	renewal
convergence	harmony	repetition
cooperation	honor	representation
correlation	interactions	revolution
courage	interdependence	rhythm
craftsmanship	interpretation	structure and function
creativity	invention	supply and demand
culture	justice	survival
cycles	liberty	symbiosis
defense/protection	loyalty	systems
democracy	maturity	tyranny

how to use this tool to engage *students* in identifying concepts and themes that unite the factual information they learn in class.

Concept Word Wall

Another simple way to keep classroom instruction focused on big ideas is to create a Concept Word Wall. To do this, identify the concepts, themes, or processes that will be the focus of a unit of study and post them on a wall or bulletin board. The words you choose can be specific to that unit or related to your discipline as a whole, or larger concepts that have relevance across disciplines. Ideally, your wall would contain a mixture of all three. A word wall on food webs, for example, might include unit-specific concepts like *producers* and *consumers,* broader science-related concepts like *ecosystem* and *energy,* and universal concepts like *renewal* and *cycle.*

Posting core concepts in an easily visible location serves to keep them front and center in your mind as you teach; it also makes students aware of the big ideas that are important to define, pay attention to, and come to understand deeply. Once the words are up, refer to and interact with them regularly—and encourage students to do the same. Show students how the words on the wall function as "conceptual Velcro," holding the facts and details from the unit together. Visit (and have students visit) the wall to link specific details or examples to larger concepts, add definitions, and identify connections between concepts. Using the wall in this way helps to grow students' understanding of both the individual concepts and the unit topic as a whole.

Essential Questions

A third way of framing your curriculum around important ideas is to use essential questions (EQs). Essential questions are open-ended questions that reflect the big ideas we want our students to come to understand. Rather than being designed to yield a single or final "correct" answer, essential questions are designed to stimulate thinking, spark discussion and debate, and raise additional questions for further inquiry. As such, they support one of the primary goals of a modern education, which is "to awaken, not 'stock' or 'train' the mind" (Wiggins, 1989, p. 46).

The following list shows examples of EQs in different content areas (McTighe, 2016). Notice how organizing your curriculum around questions like these encourages students to explore—and ensures teaching and learning stay focused on—core concepts rather than isolated facts and details.

- Dance: *In what ways can motion evoke emotion?*
- Geography: *How* where *we live influence* how *we live?*
- Government: *How should we balance the rights of individuals with the common good?*
- Health/nutrition: *What should we eat?*
- History: *Whose "story" is this?*
- Instrumental music: *If practice makes perfect, what makes "perfect" practice?*

- Literature: *To what extent can fiction reveal truth?*
- Mathematics: *When is the "correct" answer not the best solution?*
- Reading/language arts: *How do you read between the lines?*
- Science: *How are science and common sense related?*
- Visual and performing arts: *How does art reflect, as well as shape, culture?*
- Writing: *How do effective writers hook and hold their readers?*

Because essential questions are connected to big ideas—abstract, transferable concepts and processes—they are meant to be explored over time. As students consider the questions, discuss different "answers," and rethink their initial responses, they construct meaning and deepen their understanding of the relevant content. Over time, as their understanding deepens, we expect their responses to become more sophisticated and better reasoned.

There are many strategies for generating essential questions. One of the simplest involves identifying a big-idea understanding that you want students to develop and then generating one or more associated EQs, as shown in Figure 1.2.

FIGURE 1.2

Examples of Understandings and Companion Essential Questions

Big-Idea Understandings	Possible Essential Questions
True friendship is revealed during hard times, not happy times.	*Who is a "true friend," and how will you know?*
A muscle that contracts through its full range of motion generates greater force. Follow-through improves accuracy.	*How can you hit with greater power without losing control?*
Statistical analysis and display often reveal patterns in data, enabling us to make predictions with degrees of confidence.	*Can you predict what will happen in the future? With what level of confidence?*
Great literature from various cultures and time periods explores enduring themes and reveals recurrent aspects of the human condition.	*How can stories from other places and times be about us?*
Humans process both verbal and nonverbal messages simultaneously. Communication becomes more effective when verbal and nonverbal messages are aligned.	*What makes a great speaker?* *How can a great speech be "more than words"?*

When beginning to incorporate EQs into your repertoire, it can help to keep in mind the following tips from McTighe and Wiggins's (2013) *Essential Questions: Opening Doors to Student Understanding:*

1. Use two to four essential questions per unit to prioritize the content, enabling students to focus on a few big ideas.

2. Post your essential questions prominently around the classroom to serve as a constant reminder of their importance and to encourage revisiting.

3. Frame the questions in student-friendly and age-appropriate language to make them as accessible, relevant, and engaging as possible for the sophistication level and experiences of your students.

4. Pose follow-up questions to sustain and push student thinking—for example, *Because? What is your evidence for that? Who has a different idea? What would you say to someone who disagrees?*

One final note: the practice of generating essential questions isn't just for teachers. Because a modern education seeks to engage students in meaning making and to develop self-directed learners, students should be encouraged to develop their own questions—and to pursue the answers through active inquiry.

Summing Up

In this chapter, we made the case that a modern-day curriculum should be focused around important concepts that we want students to come to understand. But designing instruction around big ideas is only the start. If our goal is to prepare today's students for the challenges they'll face both in and out of the classroom, we need to think not only about what's worth teaching but also about how we can help students make sense of the information they acquire and apply their learning to new contexts. An effective way to help students develop the necessary thinking and meaning-making skills is to incorporate these skills into your everyday instructional design. The tools and strategies in Chapters 2 through 8, and the instructional planning processes in Chapter 9, will enable you to do just that.

2

Conceptualizing

The *What* and *Why* of Conceptualizing

In Chapter 1, we encouraged you to "think big"—to identify big ideas and conceptual understandings within your content and frame instruction around those ideas and understandings. The goal of this chapter is to help students start thinking big as well. When we talk about teaching students to think big, we don't just mean making them aware of the larger concepts and understandings that unite the factual knowledge they're acquiring in class; we mean helping them "add up" that factual knowledge to construct those bigger understandings for themselves. This skill—using facts, examples, observations, and experiences to construct an understanding of important concepts and conceptual relationships—is what we mean by *conceptualizing*.

There is a dual benefit to organizing instruction around core concepts and helping students learn to construct meaning for themselves. First, thinking conceptually stimulates active meaning making and leads to deep learning; it helps students understand and retain more of what they learn in class by allowing them to unite what would otherwise seem to be a random body of facts under larger conceptual umbrellas. Second, teachers won't always be there to identify and highlight what's important for students to understand. At higher levels of education and in the "real world," learners must be able to derive important understandings on their own ("What's the big idea here?") and independently transfer those understandings to new contexts. By helping students develop their conceptualizing skills now, we equip them to do just that. Think, for example, of how a student who comes to understand that *living things need water to survive* in a biology class could then apply that understanding across a variety of content areas—for example, to predict everything from the impact of droughts (ecology/social studies) and water pollution (ecology/agriculture/social studies) to patterns of settlement and migration (history/geography) to the importance of controlling water resources throughout history (history/geopolitics).

The *How* of Conceptualizing

The process of forming concepts and generalizations from observations and examples is as natural to humans as breathing. It's the way our minds work. Even very young children naturally look for patterns, formulate concepts, and make generalizations that help them interpret and make sense of the world around them. Picture how a toddler comes to understand the concept of the color red by looking for commonalities among red things that a parent points out. Or how a slightly older child infers from examples that there's a relationship between birthdays and cake, candles, and presents.

Despite this natural ability to induce concepts, students often struggle when teachers try to implement a concept-based approach in the classroom. Because the processes of forming concepts from examples and linking concepts to form generalizations are abstract and often unconscious, they're not processes that students necessarily know how to do on demand. The problem is compounded by the fact that students aren't commonly asked to do this kind of inductive thinking in school; in traditional instructional models, teachers typically *cover*—rather than asking students to *uncover*—conceptual definitions and understandings.

The good news is that you can overcome these challenges by building lessons that foster conceptual thinking and by structuring and scaffolding your teaching in a way that makes the relevant thinking processes more explicit and manageable for students. The following five instructional tools are designed to help you achieve these goals:

1. **Concept Attainment** challenges students to define core concepts for themselves by comparing examples and nonexamples to identify the critical attributes.

2. **Concept Definition Map** uses a visual organizer to help students construct and articulate conceptual definitions.

3. **A Study In . . .** engages students in processing factual information at the conceptual level by having them unite the facts from a topic or text under a large conceptual umbrella.

4. **Adding Up the Facts** shows students how they can cluster related facts and details to derive larger understandings and generalizations.

5. **Connect-the-Concepts** teaches students how to connect core concepts to form generalizations that are supported by facts and examples.

Concept Attainment

The value of organizing instruction around core concepts and helping students gain a deep understanding of those concepts is clear. What's sometimes less clear is *how* to help students develop this level of understanding. Teachers' natural instinct—to "teach concepts like vocabulary words, offering textbook definitions and then quizzing kids on those definitions later" (Stern, Ferraro, & Mohnkern, 2017, p. 53)—simply doesn't work, because understanding a concept involves so much more than knowing a simple, surface-level definition.

Concept Attainment, which is built on the work of Jerome Bruner (1973), encourages teachers to use a different approach—an inductive approach—to help students develop a deep understanding of critical concepts. Instead of defining concepts *for* students, teachers challenge students to define those concepts for themselves by comparing examples and nonexamples to determine the critical attributes. The process of extracting attributes from examples is fun for students because it's akin to "playing detective"; it's also effective, because it mimics the way we naturally come to understand and define new concepts.

The steps in a Concept Attainment lesson, along with a running example from a science classroom, are as follows.

1. Identify a concept that you want students to understand deeply. It should have at least one clear critical attribute. You can name the concept at the start of the lesson or wait until the end to reveal it.

Example: A science teacher used Concept Attainment to develop students' understanding of a *predator.* But instead of telling students that the target concept was *predator,* the teacher said that they'd be working to identify the attributes of a "mystery concept."

2. Develop *yes* and *no* examples of the concept. *Yes* examples should include—and be designed to help students discover—all the concept's critical attributes. *No* examples can include some or none of the critical attributes.

Example: To help students grasp the concept of a predator, the teacher developed a variety of *yes* examples, including cheetah, tiger, killer whale, and eagle. *No* examples included sloth, koala, cow, and brontosaurus.

3. Present some examples and challenge students to figure out what the *yes* examples have in common and how they differ from the *no* examples. Ask students to use their comparative analysis to develop a tentative list of the concept's critical attributes.

Example: After noticing that the *yes* examples were speedy meat eaters while the *no* examples were slow vegetarians, students put "speedy" and "meat eater" on their list of possible attributes.

4. Present additional *yes* and *no* examples. Have students use these examples to test and refine their list of critical attributes.

Example: The teacher added praying mantis and Venus flytrap to the *yes* examples, and rabbit and vulture to the *no* examples. Learning that *praying mantis* was a *yes* example supported the "meat eating" idea but led students to remove "speedy" from their list of attributes. The new *no* example of *vulture* helped students further refine their thinking, and they added "kills the animals it eats, as opposed to consuming already dead animals" to their list of attributes.

5. Help students review all the examples and develop a final and accurate list of the concept's critical attributes. Then have students define the concept in their own words, using examples and attributes from the lesson to help them.

Example: After reviewing all the examples and helping students refine their ideas, the teacher revealed that the concept students had been working to understand was *predator.* Students then defined *predator* as "an organism that kills and eats other animals."

6. Develop a task that asks students to apply and test their understanding of the concept.

Example: Students were given a new list with different animals and challenged to determine which ones were predators.

Concept Attainment is a versatile tool that can be used to help students grasp a wide variety of concepts—anything from *folktales* in a primary grade classroom to *contrast* in a graphic design class to *hydrophobicity* in chemistry. It's also a flexible tool in the sense that *yes* and *no* examples can take any format—pictures, texts, objects, and so on. An elementary teacher, for example, used pairs of *yes* and *no* images like the ones in Figure 2.1 to help students derive an understanding of *symmetry.*

FIGURE 2.1

Concept Attainment Examples for *Symmetry*

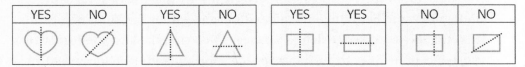

Source: From *Tools for Classroom Instruction That Works: Ready-to-Use Techniques for Increasing Student Achievement* (p. 199), by H. F. Silver, C. Abla, A. L. Boutz, and M. J. Perini, 2018, Franklin Lakes, NJ: Silver Strong & Associates/ Thoughtful Education Press and McREL International. © 2018 Silver Strong & Associates. Used with permission.

An ELA teacher used a yes-no table like the one in Figure 2.2 (p. 18) to help students discover the concept of *personification.*

To save time, look for existing texts or materials that can serve as *yes* and *no* examples rather than creating examples from scratch. A history teacher, for example, might use documents found online as the *yes* and *no* examples for a Concept Attainment lesson aimed at helping students understand the concept of a *primary source document*, as distinct from a secondary source.

FIGURE 2.2

A "Yes-No" Concept Attainment Table for *Personification*

Yes (examples of the concept)	No (nonexamples)
Money talks.	Money comes in all different denominations.
The city slowly awoke from its slumber and dressed for the day.	The population in the city has nearly doubled in the past 20 years.
The dog wept from loneliness when its owner died.	The dog got a new owner when its original owner died.
The telephone poles have been holding their arms out for a long time. They must be tired.	The telephone poles were a stain on the otherwise pristine landscape.
The wind moaned as if in pain.	His presence was as welcome as a cool breeze on a hot day.

Concept Definition Map

Defining concepts for students doesn't lead to the same level of understanding as when students construct definitions for themselves. Unfortunately, many students don't know how to craft thoughtful and thorough conceptual definitions. Concept Definition Map (adapted from Schwartz & Raphael, 1985) corrects the problem by using a visual organizer like the one in Figure 2.3 to help students understand and gather the kinds of information that are required to define a concept well (i.e., the larger category that the concept belongs to, examples of the concept, and the concept's critical attributes—especially those that distinguish it from other concepts in the same category). Completing the organizer prepares students to craft definitions in their own words that are both detailed and personally meaningful, as exemplified by the definition of *courage* that appears in Figure 2.3.

Concept Definition Maps can be used to help students deepen their understanding of familiar concepts like *courage, war, hero,* or *friendship*. They can also be used to help students develop an understanding of discipline-specific concepts that are new to them—for example, *mammal, fable, Romanticism, parallelogram,* or *argument writing*. In either case, constructing an initial definition shouldn't be the endpoint. Students should be encouraged to revise and refine their conceptual definitions over time in

FIGURE 2.3

Concept Definition Map for *Courage*

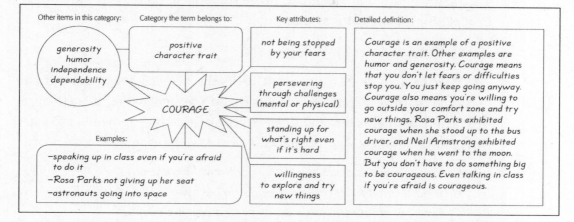

Source: From *Tools for Conquering the Common Core: Classroom-Ready Techniques for Targeting the ELA/Literacy Standards* (p. 117), by H. F. Silver and A. L. Boutz, 2015, Franklin Lakes, NJ: Silver Strong & Associates/Thoughtful Education Press. © 2015 Silver Strong & Associates. Used with permission.

light of new examples and information that they encounter—and to use the definitions that they develop to inform and evaluate future learning (e.g., Is this new person we're learning about exhibiting *courage?* Is this conflict we're studying actually a *war?*). Students should also be taught to use the tool independently—at least the idea, if not the actual organizer. Train them to develop or test their understanding of newly learned concepts by seeing if they can construct a definition that accounts for all the components on a Concept Definition Map.

A Study In . . .

In Chapter 1, we presented A Study In . . . as a tool that *teachers* could use to frame instructional units around larger, more universal concepts as opposed to simple topics. This same tool can also be employed to help *students* identify broad concepts and themes that can unite, focus, and illuminate the content they're learning. The tool trains students to do this kind of conceptualizing by helping them see the facts in terms of larger concepts.

To use the tool in this way, challenge students to review what they've learned about a topic or text and to identify a broader concept or theme that can tie the information together. Invite students to share their thinking by completing the following sentence:

I see (topic/text) as a study in (concept).

Then have students explain and justify their choices using appropriate facts and examples. Training students to add a *because* to the end of their "a study in" statements is a simple way to ensure that they remember to support those statements with evidence. Here are some examples:

- I see the *water cycle* as a study in *renewal* because . . .
- I see *Hamlet* as a study in *indecision* because . . .
- I see *our community* as a study in *cooperation* because . . .
- I see *equations* as a study in *balance* because . . .
- I see the *circulatory system* as a study in *transportation* because . . .

Encourage students to choose broader, more universal concepts that highlight a larger meaning or message, because these will provoke deeper thinking and learning than narrow or literal ones. Think how much more meaning students could extract from a lesson on the sinking of the *Titanic* by characterizing it as a study in arrogance rather than a study in icebergs! Because framing content in terms of larger concepts can be challenging, you may want to begin by having students practice with familiar topics or texts. A summer vacation might be framed as a study in *opportunity,* while *Frog and Toad Together* might be characterized as a study in *friendship*.

Once students start working with "actual" content, try giving them concepts to choose from rather than asking them to generate concepts from scratch (see Figure 1.1, p. 9, for a list of possibilities). At the end of a unit on the U.S. civil rights movement, for example, you might give students the following choice: "Do you see the civil rights movement as a study in *perseverance,* a study in *change,* a study in *conflict,* or a study in a different concept?" Besides sparking student thinking, giving students multiple concepts to choose from reinforces the idea that there's no one correct way to frame the information from a unit—that any choice is fine, as long as it can be supported.

Inviting students to view classroom content in terms of larger concepts promotes understanding and retention by requiring students to process and organize new material in a deep and personal way. It encourages students to extract larger meanings and messages instead of memorizing facts. And it facilitates connection making and transfer. In other words, it helps students both remember and think beyond the facts. Characterizing the civil rights movement as a study in perseverance, for example, would certainly help students remember key players and events. But it could also help students recognize the transferable idea that perseverance can be valuable to *any* struggle, whether personal or collective.

Adding Up the Facts

When we talk about teaching students to think more conceptually, we're talking about teaching them to change the way they think about the factual information they acquire in class—to view facts not as content to be memorized but, rather, as raw material to use in constructing important understandings. Because the skill of "thinking big"—putting facts together to see larger concepts, connections, and relationships—can be challenging for students at first, it's a skill that needs to be practiced and scaffolded.

Adding Up the Facts (McTighe, 1996a) is a tool that provides such scaffolding by inviting students to derive these kinds of understandings using a small set of carefully selected facts. To use this strategy, first identify an understanding that's worth developing ("I want students to understand that ___."). Then generate a small number of factual statements that will allow students to come to this understanding by themselves. Present the statements to students and ask them what they can infer or conclude by "adding up" the facts.

Figure 2.4 (p. 22) shows how a social studies teacher used the tool to help students derive a larger conceptual understanding from a series of simple facts as part of a unit on westward expansion.

When appropriate, help students transform their conclusions into ones that have greater transfer value by rewording them to make them less context-specific. In the example in Figure 2.4, for example, we could reword

FIGURE 2.4

Adding Up the Facts: Social Studies

Many pioneers, especially children, died from disease.

The pioneers had to grow or hunt for their food. Often, they went hungry.

Much hard work was required to settle new land—clearing fields, constructing shelter, and so on.

+ Settlers faced attacks by Native American tribes on whose lands they traveled or settled.

> **The pioneers faced many hardships in the settlement of the West.**

the conclusion as *Pioneers face many challenges and hardships.* Doing so gives us a more general relationship statement that is not specific to the context of westward expansion in America but is testable in (and ultimately transferable to) other contexts. Students could test, for example, whether that generalization holds true as they learn about the colonization and settlement of places other than the American West. That same generalization could also help them unlock content in entirely different contexts or content areas—for example, to help them predict and appreciate the hardships faced by pioneers in science, industry, or the women's rights movement.

It's worth noting that the facts students add up don't always need to be in the form of statements or sentences; images, data tables, observations, and quotations can work equally well. Moreover, the facts don't always need to be generated by you. The example in Figure 2.5 shows how primary

FIGURE 2.5

Adding Up the Facts: Science

What did we observe?
- The plant in the cabinet died.
- The plant near the window grew really well.
- The plant we put under the light grew.

What did we learn by adding up these facts?
- Plants need light to grow.

grade students generated facts for themselves by conducting an experiment on plant growth and recording their observations. They then worked as a class to add up the facts and arrive at the understanding that plants need light to grow.

If students need help putting the facts together, you can give them the important concept words that appear in the understanding you want them to generate (e.g., *pioneers* and *hardships* in the example from Figure 2.4) and instruct them to incorporate those words into their add-it-up sentences. Another scaffolding move involves "turning the tool upside down"—in other words, giving students a big idea and asking them to gather facts that support it. A "Big T" organizer like the one in Figure 2.6 is ideally suited for this purpose.

FIGURE 2.6

Big T Organizer

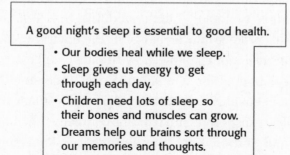

Source: From *Classroom Curriculum Design: How Strategic Units Improve Instruction and Engage Students in Meaningful Learning* (p. 32), by H. F. Silver and M. J. Perini, 2010, Franklin Lakes, NJ: Thoughtful Education Press. © 2010 Thoughtful Education Press. Used with permission.

Connect-the-Concepts

Helping students understand the individual concepts that underlie your curriculum can go a long way toward teaching them to organize and make sense of what they're learning. But helping students understand the relationships *between* and *among* concepts is also critical.

Connect-the-Concepts (adapted from work by Silver & Boutz [2015] and informed by Erickson, Lanning, & French [2017] and Stern and colleagues [2017]) engages students in comprehending these kinds of relationships by having them connect two or more concepts to form generalizations that are supported by facts from their learning. At the end of a unit on natural selection, for example, a teacher might ask students to use what they've learned to help them identify and describe a connection among the following concepts: *organism, environment, adaptation,* and *survival*. And students might connect these concepts to form the following generalization: "The degree to which an *organism* is *adapted* to its *environment* impacts its *survival*."

Generalizations are useful because they unite facts under larger understandings that can often be transferred to new contexts. The generalization above is a perfect example. Whether you're talking about biology, anthropology, literary or historical figures, or business, the relationship among environment, adaptation, and survival would be a useful one to understand. Within the context of biology, understanding that relationship would enable students to predict how a change in the environment might affect an organism's survival—for example, how climate change might impact the world's polar bear population. Outside biology, understanding that same relationship would enable students to analyze and explain the downfall of BlackBerry, a once-prosperous smartphone company that failed to adapt to the rise of iOS and Android operating systems and the changing expectations of its customers.

Using the Connect-the-Concepts tool involves five steps:

1. Pose a question that asks students to think about the relationship between two or more concepts from a topic, text, or unit of study.

Example: Within the context of an Age of Exploration unit, you might ask students if they see any relationship between *technology* and *exploration.*

2. Provide learning experiences and materials (e.g., lessons, texts, demos, hands-on activities) that will illustrate and allow students to discover the nature of that relationship for themselves.

Example: To help students discover the relationship between technology and exploration, you might have them read about technological innovations during the Age of Exploration.

3. Challenge students to connect the concepts in a sentence that describes how the concepts are related. Providing a list of "connection words" like the one in Figure 2.7 (p. 26) can help.

Example: "Advances in nautical *technology* enabled *exploration* of new places."

4. Have students use facts or examples from their learning to support or further explain the relationship they identified.

Example: "Improvements in a variety of areas, including mapmaking, shipbuilding, and navigation technology, enabled explorers to travel farther than ever before. For example, . . ."

5. Give students opportunities—immediately or over the course of the year—to reexamine and test that relationship using new examples and contexts. Does the generalization hold true more broadly? Encourage students to revise their statements as needed based on what they learn.

Example: Seeing that technological advancements facilitated exploration at multiple points in history (e.g., during the Space Race) helped students recognize that the relationship they had identified wasn't specific to nautical technology or the Age of Exploration. In response, they replaced their original relationship statement with a broader generalization: "Advances in *technology* enable *exploration* of new frontiers."

Help students understand the risks of making generalizations based on a limited number of examples and the importance of recognizing any exceptions or limitations to one's ideas. An organizer like the one in Figure 2.7 can help students express their ideas as they work. This particular organizer shows how a student responded when asked to connect the concepts of *setting, character,* and *plot* using a specific novel to inform her thinking.

To use this tool successfully, it's important to begin with a conceptual relationship that's worth having students understand—ideally, one that's transferable across examples and contexts—and to develop instructional

FIGURE 2.7

Connect-the-Concepts Organizer

Topic, Text, or Unit: *Pride and Prejudice*
Question: Is there any relationship between a story's SETTING and its CHARACTERS or PLOT?
Response/Relationship Statement (underline the connection words): The setting <u>shapes</u> characters' thoughts and actions/plot.
Explanation (use details to explain or further describe the connection or relationship): Mrs. Bennet—particularly, her obsession with marriage—provides a perfect example of how a character's thoughts and actions are shaped by the setting. At the time and place where the novel is set, women like Mrs. Bennet's daughters, who weren't independently wealthy, needed to marry well in order to do well themselves. This is why Mrs. Bennet constantly has "marriage on the mind" and takes repeated steps to try and get her daughters married.
Connection Words: If these words help you describe the connection or relationship, go ahead and use them! If not, use your own words.

Cause or lead to	Aid or contribute to	Establish	Explain or clarify
Provoke or trigger	Reveal or show	Express	Address or solve
Influence or shape	Suggest or support	Reflect	Require or depend on
Change or color	Challenge or oppose	Transform	Cooperate
Enable or allow	Increase or reduce	Determine	Characterize
Precede or follow	Enhance or promote	Regulate	Foreshadow or forecast
Make or create	Influence or guide	Reveal	Represent or symbolize

Source: Adapted from *Tools for Conquering the Common Core: Classroom-Ready Techniques for Targeting the ELA/Literacy Standards* (pp. 20 and 22), by H. F. Silver and A. L. Boutz, 2015, Franklin Lakes, NJ: Silver Strong & Associates/Thoughtful Education Press. © 2015 Silver Strong & Associates. Used with permission.

materials and experiences that will enable students to discover this relationship for themselves. If students struggle, resist the temptation to tell them how the concepts are related. (Remember, understanding must be earned!) Instead, use guiding questions to get them thinking in the right direction. For example, to help students understand that *exploration often leads to exploitation,* you might begin by presenting texts and images that illustrate this relationship. Then, to call students' attention to the relevant material, you could pose questions like these: *How were natives treated in this situation? How about here? What is being done to the land in this image? Do you see any patterns?*

Getting students to the stage where they can develop conceptual under-standings for themselves will take some work. Scaffold the skill by intro-ducing common "connection words" (see Figure 2.7 for examples) and by having students form connections between familiar items rather than com-plex concepts. For example:

> *Teacher:* Can you think of a relationship between *ladders* and *high places*?

> *Student: Ladders* <u>allow</u> people to reach *high places*.

Once students start working with actual content, you can give them fill-in-the-blank statements and have them insert appropriate connec-tion words rather than having them generate relationship statements from scratch. ("Advances in technology <u>enable</u> exploration of new fron-tiers.") Providing a list of common connection words can help, regardless of whether students are at the skill-building stage or using the tool as written. Customize the list in Figure 2.7 as needed to fit the needs of your students and the kinds of connections you want them to identify.

Summing Up

One of the differences between a novice and an expert is that experts are able to think conceptually. Thinking conceptually helps students unite what often seems to be a random body of facts and details under a larger concep-tual framework. Although the process of conceptualizing is a natural one, many students struggle when teachers implement such an approach. The practical instructional tools presented in this chapter will enable teach-ers to enhance students' ability to conceptualize by making this essential thinking process more explicit and manageable.

3

Note Making and Summarizing

The *What* and *Why* of Note Making and Summarizing

Let's begin with a simple thought experiment. Put yourself in any one of the following scenarios:

1. You are a freshman in college. It's September, and you are attending your very first college lecture. You can see right away that your professor is passionate about the subject, but boy, does she cover a lot of ground in an hour. You begin to panic that you will be unable to learn all of this material.

2. You are beginning the process of interviewing contractors for an addition to your house. Today, you are meeting the first candidate. As he explains the design options; the pricing variables; all the electrical, plumbing, HVAC, flooring, and decorative considerations; and the way one decision can affect many others, your mind starts to reel. Who knew that making a decision about your own home could be so complicated? You had better make sure you understand all of this well. After all, it's *your* money and *your* house.

3. You have been asked to serve on a school board committee to make a recommendation regarding the possible closing of two under-enrolled schools in the district. Your committee has scheduled two public hearings to listen to testimonies from interested parties, including parents, students, a few local businesses, and representatives of a Concerned Taxpayers group. Clearly, you'll need to listen carefully to the various ideas and concerns expressed in order to present a thoughtful and defensible recommendation to the board.

All three of these scenarios present common challenges that people face in school, on the job, and in life. But they're nothing you can't handle, right? Now, let's continue our thought experiment by magically taking away from you two abilities: the ability to make good notes and the ability to summarize information. What do you think of your chances for success now?

These simple scenarios help illustrate why the skills of note making and summarizing are essential to making meaning and developing solid understanding. (Note that we deliberately use the term *note making* rather than the more common *note taking* because, as we will show, good notes are created, or *made,* by the learner rather than simply *taken,* or copied from, the teacher or a text.) Without the act of making notes, the information will likely be disorganized and overwhelming. And if you take away the ability to summarize, you'll have a hard time locking anything in, making every minor detail seem as critical as the biggest of the big ideas.

Obviously, summarizing and note making are essential learning skills for success in school and in life. The goal of each is to capture, organize, and synthesize important information in order to clarify big ideas and important details. Generally speaking, note making focuses on capturing and organizing input received through listening, reading, or viewing, while summarizing is more summative in nature and is typically used *after* a particular body of content has been received. Nonetheless, both skills require the active processing of information, leading to deeper student understanding.

Research has demonstrated that both summarizing and note making have positive effects on student learning in all grade levels and content areas (Beesley & Apthorp, 2010), particularly when these skills are taught directly by teachers (Boyle, 2013; Guido & Colwell, 1987; Rahmani & Sadeghi, 2011). Both note making and summarizing support and enhance a wide range of meaning-making activities, including remembering and recalling information, reading for understanding, clarifying thoughts before writing, planning and decision making, thinking through tasks' demands and how to go about completing them, and testing and reinforcing comprehension after learning. In addition, both note making and summarizing can serve as effective formative assessment because they make students' internal thinking explicit to both the learner and the teacher.

The *How* of Note Making and Summarizing

If you take a closer look at the three scenarios that opened this chapter, you may notice that each presents a distinct challenge. The college lecture presents the challenge of *quantity,* or information overload. The home renovation scenario poses the challenge of *complexity:* because the facets of the project are interconnected, to understand any facet well you'll need to understand how it relates to all the other facets. Finally, the public hearing is predominantly a challenge of *synthesis.* To make a recommendation on possible school closings, you'll need to do more than collect factual information; you'll need to carefully consider the perspectives of various constituents, develop a nuanced understanding of the issues, and pull discrete pieces of information together into a meaningful whole.

In the remainder of this chapter, we present six practical and proven note-making and summarizing tools that help address common problems teachers experience, including students' verbatim copying of information, their inability to focus on the most important ideas, and their failure to consolidate and make sense of information. The regular use of these tools can help you create a classroom culture that builds students' comfort and competence with note making and summarizing by teaching students to construct meaning when faced with large quantities of information, informational complexity, or the need to synthesize information into a meaningful whole. These six tools are described below.

1. **Window Notes** helps teachers engage students in true *note making* (rather than *note taking*) by encouraging them to generate questions, personal reactions, and interesting connections in addition to collecting facts.

2. **Math Notes** teaches students how to analyze, plan for, and solve complex word problems.

3. **Interactive Note Making** provides students with a clear process for extracting the most important information from what they read and learn.

4. **Webbing** is a note-making format that gives students a nonlinear and visual way to make meaning and see the relationships between big ideas and supporting details within the content.

5. **4-2-1 Summarize** uses a collaborative process to help students learn how to identify essential information, construct a main idea, and write a concise summary.

6. **AWESOME Summaries** gives students an acronym-based checklist to ensure that their summaries are clear and accurate and contain the most relevant information.

Window Notes

Ask a typical student (or adult) about his or her experiences with note taking, and you'll likely get a shudder or a "Boooooooring!" in response. But we have found that these responses are based on a misconception—that taking notes amounts to copying information, which, aside from being boring, fails to engage students in the kind of active processing that meaning making requires. If the majority of classrooms reinforce the idea that notes are exercises in copying the teacher's notes or capturing verbatim what a speaker or text states, then it should come as little surprise that students put notes in the same category as taking out the garbage or cleaning their room. For far too many students, notes are nothing more than a chore.

Window Notes (Silver et al., 2018) is a tool that can help you change this dynamic. Window Notes expands students' understanding of what constitutes a note by teaching students that there is a huge difference between copying notes and actually *making* notes. At its core, this tool is an invitation to think actively, to express curiosity (a natural motivator), and to use prior knowledge and personal feelings to help construct meaning during the note-making process. Students use a window-shaped organizer that encourages them to collect four different kinds of notes:

1. *Facts:* What are the important facts and details?
2. *Questions:* What questions come to mind? What am I curious about?
3. *Connections:* How does this relate to my experiences or to other things I have learned?
4. *Feelings and reactions:* How do I feel about what I am learning?

Take a look at the Window Notes in Figure 3.1 (p. 32) made by a 4th grade student after watching a video on tornadoes.

FIGURE 3.1

Window Notes: Tornadoes

FACTS	FEELINGS & REACTIONS
• Tornadoes are rotating columns of air. They go from a thunderstorm in the sky down to the ground. • They form when warm moist air hits cool dry air. • They can reach wind speeds of 300 miles per hour.	• Tornadoes are really scary! I didn't know how much damage they could cause!
QUESTIONS	CONNECTIONS
• How do they measure the wind speed inside a tornado? • Why don't tornadoes keep going? What makes them stop?	• I saw something about a tornado on TV when my parents were watching the news. Some of the people were crying because their houses had gotten blown away. • Tornadoes remind me of getting off to school. I am trying to do so many things and I am so rushed that it feels like I am spinning at 300 miles per hour!

Source: From *Tools for Classroom Instruction That Works: Ready-to-Use Techniques for Increasing Student Achievement* (p. 161), by H. F. Silver, C. Abla, A. L. Boutz, and M. J. Perini, 2018, Franklin Lakes, NJ: Silver Strong & Associates/Thoughtful Education Press and McREL International. © 2018 Silver Strong & Associates. Used with permission.

When introducing Window Notes, help students appreciate the value of each of the four categories. Explain that recording facts helps students remember key information, generating questions enables them to clarify uncertainties and exercise their curiosity, expressing feelings and reactions makes learning personal, and making connections encourages students to tap into their prior knowledge. It is also important that students recognize that different learners will have different note-making preferences. Explain that although it is fine to have a preference, each category of notes has value. Encourage students to generate all four types of notes, even if some come less naturally than others. By getting students in the habit of thinking beyond the basics, and especially beyond the insidious practice of note copying, you'll be developing their meaning-making capacities by giving them more—and more engaging—ways to process new learning.

Math Notes

A variation on Window Notes called Math Notes (Silver, Brunsting, Walsh, & Thomas, 2012) uses the same four-pane format to develop students' ability to solve challenging word problems. Word problems are often frustrating for students because they combine reading and math skills. All too often, students try to jump to a solution rather than focusing on what they are being asked to do. Math Notes slows students down, teaching them how to use essential components of mathematical reasoning to clarify, analyze, and solve complex word problems. Specifically, students use the four panes of the Math Notes organizer to

1. Identify the *facts* of the problem, including missing information they need to figure out;

2. Clarify the *question* the problem is asking and identify any "hidden questions" the problem implies but does not state directly;

3. Create a visual *diagram* of the problem; and

4. Think through the *steps* needed to solve the problem.

Students do all of this before they actually solve the problem, making their understanding deeper, their plan clearer, and their solution more likely to be correct. A student's Math Notes appear in Figure 3.2 (p. 34). Notice how each pane in the process leads to deeper understanding of the problem and how to best solve it.

Interactive Note Making

Interactive Note Making (Boutz, Silver, Jackson, & Perini, 2012) is based on the classic SQ3R (Survey, Question, Read, Recite, and Review) reading strategy (Robinson, 1946). The tool helps students extract important information from and build deep understanding of the texts they read. It also trains students in the important skill of previewing texts for important information to build a prereading sense of what the text will be about—a habit that research shows often differentiates proficient readers from average readers (Pressley, 2006). But the benefits do not stop there: this tool also builds important study and self-monitoring skills. To use this powerhouse of a tool, follow these steps:

1. Teach students how to actively preview the section or chapter they are responsible for reading by examining the section headings, opening and

FIGURE 3.2

Math Notes: Analyzing a Word Problem

There are six 4th grade classes at Roosevelt Elementary School. All the classes have 24 students, except for one, which has 25 students. All the 4th grade students are going on a field trip to the zoo. If vans hold 8 students and buses hold 45, determine how many buses and how many vans will be needed to transport all the 4th graders to the zoo.

The Facts	The Steps
What are the facts? -Vans hold 8 people. -Buses hold 45 people. **What is missing?** -Number of kids in 4th grade -Number of vans and buses grade 4 needs.	**What steps can we take to solve the problem?** - Find out how many people are going on the trip. - See how many will fit in buses because buses hold more people and fewer vehicles make less pollution for the environment. - Put the leftover in vans. - Count the number of vehicles used
The Question	The Diagram
What question needs to be answered? -How many vans and buses does our grade need? **Are there any hidden questions that need to be answered?** -How many people are going on the trip? -Are empty seats ok? -Should each vehicle be full?	**How can we represent the problem visually?** = 8 = 145 = 45

The Solution

Source: From *Note Taking to Notemaking: How Making Notes and Summarizing Strengthen Student Learning* (p. 11), by Thoughtful Education Press, 2007, Ho-Ho-Kus, NJ: Author. © 2007 Thoughtful Education Press. Used with permission.

summarizing paragraphs, topic sentences, boldface terms, images, and end-of-chapter review questions.

2. Ask students (or work with them) to convert each section heading or subheading into a question. Have students record these questions in the Questions column (see Figure 3.3).

3. As students read the chapter, encourage them to keep these questions in mind and to collect notes that address the questions.

4. When students are finished reading and making notes, instruct them to check their understanding and retention of the material by folding the organizer so that the questions are visible, but their notes are covered up. Students should generate a response to each question without peeking at their notes.

5. Ask students to open up their organizer to check their responses against their notes. Students should actively assess their understanding by making one of the following marks:

✓ = I know this.

★ = I need to review this.

? = I have a question about this (students should record their questions).

Figure 3.3 depicts a middle school student's notes made using the Interactive Note Making technique.

FIGURE 3.3

A Student's Notes Using Interactive Note Making

QUESTIONS	MAIN IDEAS	SUPPORTING DETAILS	MONITOR
What is the function of blood?	Brings food and oxygen to cells and carries away wastes. It also carries hormones, proteins, and infection fighters to where they're needed.		★
What are the components of blood?	Red blood cells, white blood cells, platelets, and plasma		✓
What is plasma?	Cells travel through the blood in a yellowish fluid called plasma.	Plasma is approx. 90% water.	★
What is the function of white blood cells?	White blood cells (WBCs) help the body fight infection and disease.	White blood cells can destroy infected cells and make antibodies.	? What's an antibody?

Source: From *Tools for Thoughtful Assessment: Classroom-Ready Techniques for Improving Teaching and Learning* (p. 110), by A. L. Boutz, H. F. Silver, J. W. Jackson, and M. J. Perini, 2012, Franklin Lakes, NJ: Silver Strong & Associates/Thoughtful Education Press. © 2012 Silver Strong & Associates. Used with permission.

In this description of Interactive Note Making, we have focused our attention on reading, but this tool works equally well for classroom presentations, lectures, and videos. To use it for these applications, provide students with the essential questions you want them to focus their attention on, and then encourage them to use the organizer to collect relevant information during the lesson and test their understanding afterward.

Webbing

Webbing is a note-making process by which students can visually represent key ideas from a presentation or a text. It is an exceptional meaning-making enhancer for several reasons. First, webs are nonlinear, allowing students to capture and organize their thinking freely, so they can put more of their mind's attention on processing and capturing information and less on adhering to the format associated with traditional outlining. Second, webbing's graphic format makes low-level copying impossible. Instead, students have to make meaning by converting the content of what they are reading or hearing into *visual* chunks, with important ideas quite literally connected to the details that support them. Thus, webs are particularly well suited to helping students represent relationships among facts and concepts. For example, the web in Figure 3.4 was developed by a student while reading a section from her science textbook on the human nervous system.

Besides helping kids organize and make sense of information, webs are also great tools for brainstorming ideas, as illustrated in Figure 3.5 (p. 38). To create this web, a group of students generated their collective ideas (and later tested them) in response to a physics challenge: "How can you get 30 pennies to float on water using only aluminum foil?"

Another use of webs is as a review and study aid. To use webs in this way, challenge students to create a web as a self-test on a lesson or topic. Can they create a web that captures the big ideas of the content? Can they recall the key details that support each big idea? In comparing their web with their notes or textbook, which parts of the content do they know well, and what might they need to go back and review further?

FIGURE 3.4

A Web for Collecting Important Information (from a Reading)

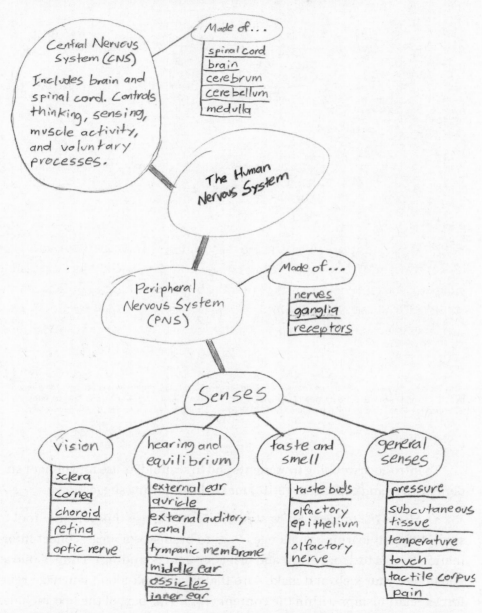

FIGURE 3.5

A Web for Brainstorming

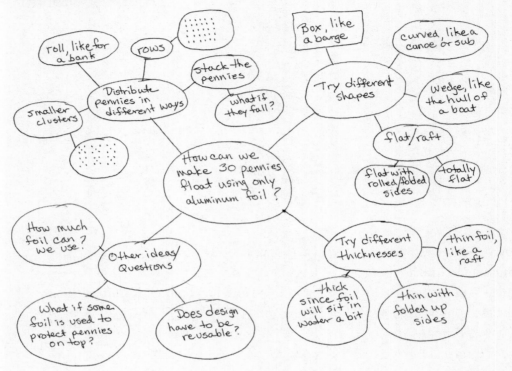

Source: From *Tools for Classroom Instruction That Works: Ready-to-Use Techniques for Increasing Student Achievement* (p. 156), by H. F. Silver, C. Abla, A. L. Boutz, and M. J. Perini, 2018, Franklin Lakes, NJ: Silver Strong & Associates/ Thoughtful Education Press and McREL International. © 2018 Silver Strong & Associates. Used with permission.

To introduce webbing to students and to scaffold its use for younger students, Silver and colleagues (2018) make the following suggestions:

- *Model the process.* Show students how you use this versatile tool to solve different learning challenges (e.g., to brainstorm ideas, collect information from a text, or review and test your understanding). Think aloud as you create your web, and make sure that your think-aloud language reinforces relationships within the content (e.g., "This part of the text includes all the details that support the subtopic I just wrote over here: *how the Pyramids were built*. So I'll add them to that part of my web, like this.").

- *Allow primary-grade students to skip subtopics.* Simply give them a single central topic and let them record everything they know or learn about it around the central topic circle.

- *Provide the subtopics.* For example, if students are learning about the artist Georgia O'Keefe, create a starter web for them with *Georgia O'Keefe* at the center and the subtopics branching off. Consider turning each subtopic into a question (e.g., *What was Georgia O' Keefe's childhood like? What inspired her to become an artist? What is so interesting about her paintings? What are some of her most famous paintings?*). To complete the web, students collect important details that answer each question.

4-2-1 Summarize

One of the biggest challenges students face in summarizing information is determining which information should be included in a summary and which information can be left out. What matters most? What are the biggest of the big ideas? Which are the essential details that support those big ideas, and which are trivial or negligible?

4-2-1 Summarize (Boutz et al., 2012) uses a collaborative learning process to teach students how to separate essential from nonessential information, construct main ideas, and synthesize and summarize what they've learned in writing. After reading a text or engaging in a learning experience, students review the text or lesson and decide what they believe are four very important ideas or points. Working individually, students record their four big ideas on an organizer (see Figure 3.6, p. 40). Note that asking students to pick out four important ideas is different from asking them to state the main idea, which is often difficult for students to do without a process to get there. The rest of the steps in this tool provide that process.

Each student then pairs up with another student to share and compare ideas. Each pair discusses both students' ideas and strives to reach consensus on the two most important ideas. Then, each student pair teams up with another pair to form a group of four; together, the four students share and compare their ideas and then work as a team to determine the single most important idea in the text or learning experience. Through this process (four ideas generated individually, two ideas negotiated within student pairs, one big idea negotiated among a team of four), students distill their thinking until their learning contains the essential information—and only the essential information.

This process engages students in collaborative meaning making and prepares them to develop a succinct summary of the text. Students' most important idea typically serves as a topic sentence, and the ideas that they collected and refined during the process usually provide strong supporting details. Figure 3.6 shows how the process played out in a middle school classroom. Notice how, in winnowing ideas down from four to two, this student and her partner kept one of her original ideas (*The population gets*

FIGURE 3.6

4-2-1 Summarize: Student Organizer and Written Summary

FOUR key ideas	When gold is discovered, people from around the world rush to California.	The population gets bigger and more diverse—but the native population drops.	New towns, businesses, roads, and schools are developed.	Mining for gold destroys the environment.
The TWO most important ideas		The population gets bigger and more diverse—but the native population drops.	The land is developed but also destroyed.	
The ONE most important idea		The Gold Rush changed the population and landscape of California.		

Summary Paragraph: *What did I learn?*

The Gold Rush changed both the population and the landscape of California. When gold was discovered at Sutter's Mill in 1848, people from the United States and around the world rushed to California. The overall population got larger and more diverse. But the native population dropped. Over 100,000 natives were killed or died from disease or starvation. The rush to California didn't just change the population. It changed the landscape, too. Towns, businesses, roads, and schools sprang up everywhere. And miners polluted and destroyed the environment. Overall, the Gold Rush changed California's land, people, and development in many different and lasting ways.

bigger and more diverse—but the native population drops) and combined some of the other original ideas to form a bigger idea (*The land is developed but also destroyed*). Then, as a team of four, students constructed the one most important idea that captured the essence of all the ideas.

AWESOME Summaries

Summarizing is an effective meaning-making strategy because it requires students to process and synthesize information. But many students don't know how to craft a high-quality summary. AWESOME Summaries (Silver & Boutz, 2015) addresses this problem by providing students with an easy-to-remember acronym that defines the critical attributes of an effective summary. Students can use the AWESOME acronym as a checklist before they write their summaries (i.e., to plan); during the writing process (as guidelines for developing their summaries); and after they have written their summaries (to review and refine their work):

A: Is the information in my summary *accurate?*

W: Has the length of the original material been *whittled down* significantly?

E: Did I include *enough information* to capture the essence of the original material?

S: Is the information in my summary logically organized and *sequenced?*

O: Did I give an *objective* (free from personal opinions) summary of the original material?

M: Did I summarize the original material in *my own words?*

E: Does my summary contain the *essential ideas only?* Did I eliminate unnecessary details?

Summing Up

There is no doubt that students who are adept at making notes and summarizing information have a far better chance at achieving success in school and beyond. Through note making and summarizing, students make meaning by capturing, organizing, and synthesizing information so that big ideas and essential details are clear. The primary goal of this chapter has been to offer simple tools that help students become better at both of these essential meaning-making skills. However, there has been a secondary goal as well: to change students' mindsets and help them overcome the common perception that notes and summarizing are boring and, instead, to help them see that both skills are powerful and personally meaningful learning processes.

4

Comparing

The *What* and *Why* of Comparing

Take a look at the two images in Figure 4.1.

Put aside for a moment the alarm bells that may be going off in your teacher brain when you see a classroom like the one on the right. What we're especially interested in here is not your take on the classroom management or pedagogical skills of the teachers depicted. What we're interested in is your thinking process. What's going on in your mind? How are you processing these two photographs? What are you thinking? What "meanings" are you making?

By juxtaposing these two images, we are tapping into a natural human capacity. People are hardwired to compare; the act of considering items side by side (either physically or, more typically, mentally) and analyzing them

FIGURE 4.1

A Tale of Two Classrooms

for similarities and differences is a fundamental meaning-making skill. It's what enables you to quickly recognize the common features indicating that both images are classrooms while simultaneously pushing obvious differences directly into the beam of your attention.

Comparing is also, academically speaking, one of the highest-impact skills. Meta-analytic studies (Dean, Hubbell, Pitler, & Stone, 2012; Marzano, Pickering, & Pollock, 2001) have shown that teaching students how to compare and contrast leads to significant gains in achievement. Hattie and Donoghue (2016) note the critical role of comparative thinking in developing transfer, observing that "transfer is a major outcome of learning and is more likely to occur if students are taught how to detect similarities and differences between one situation and a new situation before they try to transfer their learning to the new situation" (p. 4). Notice a key idea from these researchers—*teaching students how*. Although comparing is a natural skill, using it at a high level is another thing entirely. If we expect students to master the skill of comparative analysis and reap the academic benefits that can come with it, then we need to provide "explicit instruction in the use of processes associated with identifying similarities and differences" (Dean et al., 2012, p. 121).

When learners engage in purposeful comparison, they are constructing meaning and growing their understanding during the learning process. Comparing is a foundational thinking skill and a necessary underpinning to more complex processes such as argumentation, decision making, and problem solving. For example, if your goal is to teach students how to craft high-quality arguments, the learning process should involve comparison—having students analyze sample written arguments to determine what they have in common and to zero in on key differences that distinguish their claims, evidence, and reasons. The same is true for almost any higher-order thinking goal or task. If we want students to make good decisions, then they need to be able to compare and contrast alternatives. If we want them to conduct an inquiry or design a product that solves a problem, we can be sure that competing ideas and multiple possibilities will present themselves along the way; thus, the ability to think comparatively will be essential to their success.

The *How* of Comparing

As beneficial as comparing can be, many teachers report that their experience using it doesn't always produce the kinds of learning outcomes suggested by the research. In our many years of helping teachers develop students' thinking skills, we have found that certain common and identifiable pitfalls, or problems of practice, can occur when students are asked to compare. The six tools discussed in this chapter have been selected (and, in some cases, developed) specifically to help teachers overcome these problems of practice. Figure 4.2 identifies some of the most common challenges that teachers and students face when conducting comparisons, and summarizes how each tool can address these problems.

FIGURE 4.2

Common Comparison Pitfalls and Tools That Address Them

The Pitfall, or Problem of Practice	The Tool(s) That Address the Pitfall
Students rush into the comparison without a deep understanding of the items they're comparing or identifying the salient dimensions to be compared.	1. **Describe First, Compare Second** teaches students to describe each item thoroughly before looking for similarities and differences.
Students' comparisons focus on trivial details of the items under investigation.	2. **Meaningful and Manageable Criteria** teaches students how to focus their attention on important aspects of the items under investigation.
Students don't have an effective way to organize their findings as they conduct their comparison.	3. **Top Hat Organizer** and **Comparison Matrix** provide students with visual organizers that guide thinking— and that are superior to the Venn diagram.
Students' comparisons don't go anywhere; students walk away without having made any conclusions or generalizations as a result of their comparison.	4. **What Can You Conclude?** challenges students to build deeper understanding by making and supporting conclusions about the items they've compared. 5. **Compare and Conclude Matrix** enables students to review their comparative process and draw a conclusion or make a decision based on their analysis. It is especially useful when students are asked to compare more than two items.
Students don't transfer their understanding of comparative thinking to other contexts (e.g., classroom discussions).	6. **Community CIRCLE** encourages teachers and students to apply the power of comparative thinking to classroom discussions.

Describe First, Compare Second

One of the biggest obstacles to effective comparing is that many students rush headlong into the process without a clear understanding of what they are actually being asked to compare and for what purpose. Describe First, Compare Second (Silver & Boutz, 2015) is designed to slow students down, requiring them to examine the items closely instead of rushing to find similarities and differences. The effectiveness of the tool is enhanced in several ways. First, students need to clarify the reason for making a comparison. Then they identify and describe the most salient aspects or dimensions of the items to be compared. When first using this tool, the teacher may provide students with the comparative dimensions; as students become more proficient in the process, they can and should be encouraged to identify the dimensions on their own.

Clearly delineated dimensions of the items under investigation are essential to guide the comparison; without them, students often end up with a grab bag of information about each item, much of it unrelated or trivial (e.g., *Abraham Lincoln was very tall and had a beard. George Washington wore a white wig and chopped down a cherry tree. Abraham Lincoln is on the five-dollar bill. George Washington is on the one-dollar bill.*). But when students collect information about (1) each president's key accomplishments, (2) the biggest challenge each faced, and (3) how each became president, their thinking becomes focused on what matters most.

The structure of this tool further enhances meaning making by incorporating a simple, three-column description organizer that allows students to line up the relevant information about each item side by side. Figure 4.3 shows a Description Organizer completed by a student who was examining linear equations and quadratic equations.

Notice that the student has not yet identified any similarities and differences, only developed a strong description of each item. Having thoroughly "described first" in this way, the student is in a far better position to pick out important similarities and differences between the items—to "compare second." Of course, it is always a good idea to model both the describing and the comparing processes before asking students to do them. Try using

FIGURE 4.3

Description Organizer: Linear Equations and Quadratic Equations

— Description Organizer —

Item or text #1: _Linear equations_	Describe these attributes, aspects, or components:	Item or text #2: _Quadratic equations_
$y = ax + b$	Standard Equation	$y = ax^2 + bx + c$
Select random values for x. Substitute and evaluate for y. Plot ordered pairs (x, y). Plot point b on the y axis to determine y intercept. Use slope (a) to determine additional points.	How to solve	Select random values for x. Substitute x and evaluate for y. Plot ordered pairs (x, y). A more complex process called completing the square is used to determine the vertex of the parabola and its general shape.
straight line	Shape of graph	Parabola
- infinite number of ordered pairs that make the equation true - given y, there is only one x value that makes the equation true.	Solution	- Infinite number of pairs that make the equation true. - Given y, there can be 0, 1, or 2 x values that make the equation true.

Source: From *Tools for Classroom Instruction That Works: Ready-to-Use Techniques for Increasing Student Achievement* (p. 189), by H. F. Silver, C. Abla, A. L. Boutz, and M. J. Perini, 2018, Franklin Lakes, NJ: Silver Strong & Associates/ Thoughtful Education Press and McREL International. © 2018 Silver Strong & Associates. Used with permission.

common items that students will be able to describe and compare readily, such as knife and fork, hot dog and hamburger, soccer and hockey, and so on.

Over time, students will internalize this important "describe first, compare second" habit, thereby gaining an important and transferable skill that will help them become more strategic comparative thinkers.

Meaningful and Manageable Criteria

As students become more comfortable with the process of describing and comparing, you can and should challenge them to identify the important dimensions or aspects of the items to be compared. As a starting point, use familiar items to engage students in clarifying the purpose of making a comparison and then determining the key aspects to be considered. For example, a teacher might say, "Imagine that your family wants a pet and is considering a dog or a cat. How would you go about deciding? What criteria would you use to compare cats and dogs?" After the class collects and discusses students' ideas, the teacher says, "OK. So far, we have easy to care for, life span, and fun to play with. What else can we think of?" A student says, "Behavior." The teacher responds, "Interesting. Why do you think behavior is an important aspect to examine?" In this way, the teacher challenges the class to reach consensus on a set of manageable and meaningful criteria to guide the comparison process.

After students have had some practice clarifying the purpose of the comparison and determining criteria to consider, you can engage them in more academic comparisons and continue to spur their thinking about what's worth comparing: "What are some important aspects to focus on as we examine bacteria and viruses? Why? What makes these aspects important? Can we reach agreement as a class on the three or four most important aspects that we'll examine?" Over time, shift this responsibility entirely to students: "To conduct your comparison of photosynthesis and cellular respiration, you will be selecting four or five common elements to compare. You will also be asked to explain why you chose the elements that you did."

This undertaught skill of clarifying the criteria for comparison can be crucial to students' academic success, especially on standardized tests, where comparative reading tasks are common. Sometimes, these comparative tasks provide or suggest the criteria students should focus on, as in this example: "Compare the kinds of adaptations that enable the animals you read about to survive in their various habitats. You may wish to address adaptations involved in finding food, regulating body temperature, or avoiding predators" (Silver & Boutz, 2015, p. 26).

Other times, students are entirely on their own when it comes to choosing the criteria around which to focus their comparison. To prepare students for success on these kinds of test items, provide them with sample tasks, both with and without criteria. When tasks provide criteria, teach students to zero in on them. For tasks that don't provide criteria, talk through the meaningful elements that students might want to consider. For example, if an item asks students to compare two characters, students might choose to focus on their personalities, experiences, or interactions with other people. A criterion like physical appearance, by contrast, is typically less relevant to understanding a character's traits.

Top Hat Organizer and Comparison Matrix

The most common organizer that teachers use to help students identify similarities and differences is the Venn diagram. However, we recommend using a Top Hat organizer instead. Unlike a Venn diagram, a Top Hat offers students plenty of room to record both similarities and differences. Moreover, with a Top Hat, students can line up important differences next to one another. This parallelism is not possible with a Venn diagram, whose middle separates the differences. Figure 4.4 shows how a student used Top Hat to identify important differences and similarities between two literary movements, Realism and Naturalism.

FIGURE 4.4

Top Hat Organizer: Realism and Naturalism

Differences	
Unique to Realism	**Unique to Naturalism**
• Belief that people's freedom of choice is limited by outside forces • Attempts to represent life faithfully and accurately • Tends to downplay plot in favor of character Key authors and texts: • Henry James: _Daisy Miller_ • Mark Twain: _The Adventures of Huckleberry Finn_ • William Dean Howells: "Editha"	• Belief that outside forces control human behavior; there is no free will • Attempts to show how the struggle to survive against outside forces is heroic • Tends to create literary characters that the reader feels sorry for Key authors and texts: • Stephen Crane: _Maggie: A Girl of the Streets_, "The Open Boat" • Frank Norris: "The Octopus"

Similarities
• Both tend to focus on common, everyday people. • Both believe that outside forces influence how humans behave. • Both are reactions against Romanticism, which celebrates individualism and free will.

Another recommended organizer for developing comparative-analysis skills is a simple Comparison Matrix. This tool makes a critical aspect of the comparison process explicit by including a place to identify the specific dimensions to be compared, thus ensuring that students' comparisons don't wander down irrelevant paths. Like the Top Hat, it also provides more space to record ideas than is typically available on a Venn diagram. Figure 4.5 shows an example.

FIGURE 4.5

Comparison Matrix: Tundra and Desert

| Dimensions for Comparison: | Tundra | | Desert |
	Unique Characteristics	Similar to Both	Unique Characteristics
CLIMATE	frigid temperatures	harsh, inhospitable	hot and dry
TOPOGRAPHY	permafrost	treeless plain	sand
VEGETATION		minimal (unable to survive)	
NATURAL RESOURCES		oil, natural gas	
POPULATION		few permanent residents, nomads	

What Can You Conclude?

One reason students extract little meaning or build only superficial understanding when making comparisons is that teachers often move on right after asking students to identify similarities and differences. What should be a catalyst for deep thinking becomes a lost opportunity. Worse yet, it leaves our students with the impression that comparing is merely an exercise in tallying—in listing similarities and differences. What Can You

Conclude? is a technique that ensures deep thinking when students make comparisons. At the heart of this tool is a rich question that forces students to look back on the items they compared and make a generalization or draw a conclusion. Some examples of such questions follow:

- Are spiders and insects more similar or more different?
- What do you think is the most important difference between the two fables we read?
- Based on your comparison of Booker T. Washington's and W. E. B. Du Bois's positions on education, who do you think makes the more compelling argument?
- Why do you think that some students prefer to work with fractions and others prefer to work with decimals? Which do you prefer?

Depending on your instructional objectives, you may have students develop their conclusions in writing, through small-group conversation, through whole-class discussion, or through a combination of these formats. No matter the format, remind students that they should review what they have learned about the items before drawing their conclusion. The goal is for students to be able to explain and justify their conclusions by citing specific information that they have gathered through the comparative-analysis process.

You can take students' thinking even further by asking them to apply their learning or transfer it to a new situation via a task. The following task ideas from various comparison lessons are adapted from *Compare & Contrast* (Silver, 2010, pp. 47–48):

- Create a "Flip Strip" that shows how frogs and toads differ.
- Write a simple thesis essay that argues either for or against this statement: *The heroes in tall tales are like today's superheroes.*
- Compare the rates and terms of two banks' certificates of deposit (CDs)—one offering simple interest and one offering compound interest. What conclusions can you draw? Which is the better choice?
- Create an exercise and conditioning program that incorporates both aerobic and anaerobic activities.
- Write a poem about an unjust situation from today's times. Use the style of one of the poems we studied.

Compare and Conclude Matrix

A Compare and Conclude Matrix is a modification of the Comparison Matrix (see Figure 4.5) with two noteworthy features added: (1) the capacity to compare more than two items, and (2) a space that requires students to draw a conclusion or make a decision based on their comparison.

Let's play out an elementary-level example using four common fruits: apples, oranges, grapes, and bananas. First, we'll start with the purpose: imagine that we have the opportunity to start a fruit farm in western Maryland and need to decide which fruit to grow to sell in the wholesale market. We'll need to consider the key criteria for comparing our four fruits with our purpose in mind. Figure 4.6 shows how a Compare and Conclude Matrix could be used for this example. Notice that the matrix includes five key criteria associated with the purpose of the comparison (namely, to reach a decision). Given this purpose, students can use these evaluative criteria in a variety of ways to help them reach their decision. For example, students might use the criteria to collect the relevant information about each fruit, or they might numerically rate each fruit based on how well it meets

FIGURE 4.6

Compare and Conclude Matrix: Four Fruits

Criteria / Items to Be Compared	Suitability to Region	Cost to Plant	Cost to Grow (e.g., Water, Fertilizer)	Cost to Harvest	Wholesale Market Price
APPLES					
ORANGES					
GRAPES					
BANANAS					

Conclusion

each criterion (e.g., using a five-point scale, with 5 being most favorable and 1 being least favorable). Equally important, the matrix requires students to look over the results and make a final decision based on their comparative analysis. Using this matrix, one student group wrote the following in the conclusion box: "After our research and comparison of the four fruits against the criteria, we decided that apples would be the best fruit to plant on our inherited land in western Maryland."

Note that the conclusion students make can take various forms. For example, students might use the conclusion box to reach a decision (as in the fruit farm example above) or form a generalization (e.g., "The three main characters were all shy, yet courageous.").

Community CIRCLE

Comparing is not merely a cognitive skill to be applied to specific tasks and lessons; it is an essential way of thinking that almost always leads to deeper understanding. Take classroom discussions as an example. During good classroom discussions, students generate a wide variety of responses. Too often, though, these responses go unexplored and remain a hodgepodge of scattered ideas. Bringing comparative thinking into the mix can change that.

Community CIRCLE (Silver, Perini, & Boutz, 2016) is a tool that increases participation in classroom discussions by encouraging students to draw on their own experiences and express their own opinions. Once students have generated a pool of ideas, the tool harnesses the power of comparison to help students see the big ideas, make generalizations, and derive insights from the wide range of responses generated. It uses the acronym *CIRCLE* to lay out the steps teachers follow to implement it in the classroom. Figure 4.7 (p. 54) outlines these steps and shows how a teacher used them to guide a classroom discussion.

Here are suggestions for making the most of Community CIRCLE:

• Make sure that your discussion is tied to a concrete purpose or learning goal, and keep this goal in mind as you develop the prompt, design the task, and guide the conversation.

FIGURE 4.7

A Community CIRCLE Lesson

Create a prompt that invites students to share personal knowledge, experiences, or opinions.

The teacher uses the following prompt to get students thinking about their personal experiences with the attitude/achievement relationship: "Think of a time when your attitude has either helped or gotten in the way of your success. How did your attitude affect your success?" To prepare students for the sharing process, she has them jot down their ideas on paper before joining the circle.

Invite students to sit in a circle and share their responses.

Students arrange their chairs in a circle and begin sharing. Everyone is required to participate.

Review key ideas by having students summarize each other's responses.

Students restate or summarize their classmates' ideas, making sure to refer to each other by name.

Compare ideas.

With the teacher's help, students identify similarities and differences like these:

"Taryn's and Carlos's experiences seem similar. Both spoke about how a coach helped them improve their attitude and how their improved attitude helped them get better at their sport."

"Joe and Amy had very different opinions. Amy didn't believe that her attitude affected her performance in class, but Joe was convinced that his did. He supported his belief with several specific examples, like how when he made an effort to have a more positive attitude about math, he actually started doing better in math class."

Look for patterns.

The teacher challenges students to develop generalizations about attitude that are rooted in their collective experiences. After some discussion and debate, students agree to these two generalizations: (1) Your attitude can affect your performance; (2) It's better to have a positive attitude than a negative one.

Extend student thinking.

The teacher asks students to read the classic American poem "Casey at the Bat" and look for evidence that supports and/or refutes their generalizations about attitude.

Source: From *Tools for a Successful School Year (Starting on Day One): Classroom-Ready Techniques for Building the Four Cornerstones of an Effective Classroom* (p. 37), by H. F. Silver, M. J. Perini, and A. L. Boutz, 2016, Franklin Lakes, NJ: Silver Strong & Associates/Thoughtful Education Press. © 2016 Silver Strong & Associates. Used with permission.

- Before conducting a Community CIRCLE, teach or reinforce positive discussion behaviors, such as listening carefully, disagreeing respectfully, and addressing classmates by name.
- When you present the prompt, encourage students to slow down their thinking, search their memories deeply, and collect their ideas in writing before joining the discussion.
- Vary your prompts. Among other options, you can create prompts that help students explore concepts ("What does prejudice mean to you?"),

analyze causes or effects ("What makes a story engaging?" or "What if there were no fractions and decimals and we could use only whole numbers? How would our lives change?"), or evaluate decisions ("Was it the right decision to retire the space shuttle program? Why or why not?").

Use Community CIRCLE regularly so that it—and the thinking and collaborative behaviors it embodies—becomes part of your classroom culture.

Summing Up

Comparing is a natural human thinking process that is essential to making meaning. It has also been recognized as one of the highest-impact skills for raising student achievement. However, many teachers find that using comparison in the classroom does not lead to the kinds of results outlined in the research. We have found that the biggest reason for this disconnect is that there are common and identifiable "problems of practice" that prevent comparison from reaching its full potential in the classroom. With the tools in this chapter, teachers can directly address these challenges and realize the great potential of comparing as a meaning-making skill that helps all students become better learners and thinkers.

5

Reading for Understanding

The *What* and *Why* of Reading for Understanding

When we think of the ability to read for understanding—to extract important information from texts and support interpretations with textual evidence—the word we can't stop thinking about is the word *so*. Not in the "who cares?" sense of that word, but rather its opposite.

Allow us to explain. Like all educators, we care deeply about reading for understanding because it is *so* central to learning and meaning making that its importance cannot be overstated; because the research on reading for understanding is *so* clear that students who are adept at it will always achieve at higher levels than their peers who are not; because teaching students how to develop this skill is *so* important that every teacher, regardless of grade level or content area, needs to make it a priority.

Although there are a great number of strategies and even entire programs dedicated to enhancing students' reading comprehension, we have chosen to focus on a specific set of practical and proven tools and strategies for helping all readers develop the skills that the most proficient readers use to make meaning when they read. At the heart of the approach is the recognition, borne out by a large body of research, that proficient reading involves three distinct phases that lead to deep understanding. Reading expert Michael Pressley (2006) puts it this way: "In general, the conscious processing that is excellent reading begins before reading, continues during reading, and persists after reading is completed" (p. 57).

The *How* of Reading for Understanding

This chapter focuses on the *how* of teaching students to use the three phases of proficient reading—before reading, during reading, and after reading—to make meaning from text. Specifically, we present five tools and strategies that teachers can use to target and grow the skills associated with all three phases of proficient reading:

1. **Power Previewing** teaches students how to conduct a "power-skim" to build a prereading sense of a text's content and structure.

2. **Scavenger Hunt** uses the well-known scavenger hunt game format to engage students in active searches for key information in the texts they read.

3. **Single-Sentence Summaries** gets students in the proficient-reader habit of stopping regularly during reading and creating quick summaries to consolidate understanding.

4. **Reading Stances** helps students to build deep understanding and dynamic interpretations by teaching them how to examine and respond to texts through multiple lenses, or "stances."

5. **Reading for Meaning** is a comprehensive reading strategy that incorporates all three phases of proficient reading—*before, during,* and *after* reading—to engage students in the active construction of meaning from beginning to end.

Power Previewing

Highly proficient readers don't just open texts and start reading; they preview texts, and they prepare themselves to read those texts deeply and well. Power Previewing engages all students in this proficient-reader habit, helping them activate their prior knowledge, build a prereading sense of what the text is about, and create a conceptual framework into which new information gathered through reading can be integrated.

Silver and Boutz (2015) have developed a simple, teachable set of proficient-reader behaviors to help students conduct a Power Preview. To make the behaviors more memorable for students, each begins with the letter *P*, as shown in Figure 5.1 (p. 58).

FIGURE 5.1

The Five *P*s of Power Previewing

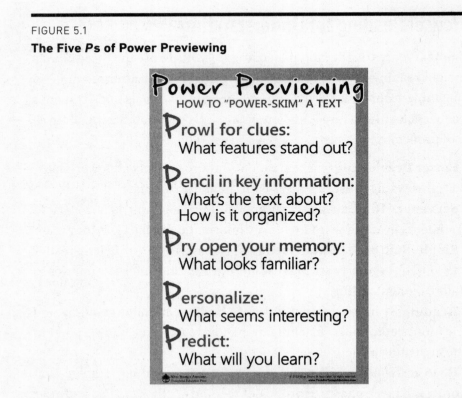

Source: Power Previewing (Poster) by Silver Strong & Associates, 2018, Franklin Lakes, NJ: Author. © 2018 Silver Strong & Associates. Used with permission.

When introducing this tool to students, place special attention on the first *P, Prowl for clues,* by making sure that you teach students what to look for when skimming for important information and notable text features. For nonfiction texts, for example, students should be trained to look for the following features, which typically convey important information:

- Titles and headings
- Opening paragraphs/introductions
- Summary paragraphs/lists of key points
- Bold, italicized, underlined, or highlighted words and phrases
- Visual information (e.g., graphs, maps, tables, pictures)
- Captions
- Start-of-chapter and end-of-chapter questions

As with all reading strategies, teacher modeling is key. Explain to students why Power Previewing is important and how it helps improve comprehension and engagement. Use sample texts to show students how you work through the five *P*s, and give students repeated opportunities to Power Preview texts—making sure that you bring students back to their previews after reading to reflect on how their prereading ideas and predictions played out.

Scavenger Hunt

Scavenger Hunt (Silver & Boutz, 2015) is an instructional tool created to help students read more actively and purposefully. To increase student engagement, the tool incorporates an element of play by inviting students to think of a text as a search for specific items, information, or features that students have to find and then demonstrate that they have found. Scavenger Hunt allows teachers to target specific standards-based reading skills by designing different types of search tasks. Figure 5.2 (p. 60) shows how teachers can design search tasks that require students to practice common skills that all reading standards emphasize.

Once you have designed your search tasks for a particular text, follow these steps to engage all students in a text-based Scavenger Hunt:

1. Provide students with a copy of the text and the search tasks.

2. Instruct students how to work (e.g., on their own or in "search parties") and how to mark or record their findings (e.g., by marking up the text, using sticky notes, or using a line numbering system to identify relevant passages).

3. Walk around the room, look or listen in as students work, and provide support as needed.

4. Review and discuss students' responses as a class.

5. Encourage students to defend or debate their responses, and work to build consensus when appropriate. (Sometimes one response is better supported by the text than others; other times, multiple competing responses are all equally valid. In either case, make sure students understand why this is so.)

6. Use students' responses to particular search tasks to zero in on the skills that are giving students the most trouble.

FIGURE 5.2

Scavenger Hunt Search Tasks Tied to Common Reading Skills

Reading Skill	Sample Search Tasks That Build This Skill
Search for factual /explicitly stated information.	• How did the alien communicate to Alicia that he was lost? Find the sentence or passage that tells us. • Find two examples of adaptation mentioned in the article.
Use textual evidence to support inferences/ conclusions.	• Find two words or pictures that might lead us to conclude that Frog is scared. • Find three sentences from the passage that support the following conclusion. . . .
Identify central ideas and themes.	• Find the paragraph that best reflects the main idea of this passage as a whole. • If the main idea of this passage is _____, what two details from the text best support it?
Find details that reveal key information about (or relationships between) characters, settings, events, or individuals.	• How can we tell the narrator is naïve? Find some evidence. • Find three details from the story that help establish its setting. • How did Newton's work influence Einstein's discoveries? Find some evidence.
Use textual clues that help reveal the meaning of words and phrases as they're used in the text; understand how specific words can affect tone.	• Find some details or phrases that help us understand the meaning of the word *symbiotic* as it's used in this passage. • Find words and phrases that contribute to the conversational tone of this article.
Identify or compare text structures; explain how individual elements contribute to the larger piece.	• Find the portion of this passage that is structured chronologically. • In this article, the author presents two seemingly irreconcilable positions. How does she show that they are not so irreconcilable after all? Find the section that achieves this reconciliation.
Find passages that reveal the author's point of view or purpose.	• Find at least three sentences that help reveal the author's point of view. • Does the author believe that the United States' military escalation during Vietnam was justified or a mistake? Find evidence to support your position.
Evaluate content presented in other formats (e.g., visually, quantitatively).	• Find a picture that shows how the hungry caterpillar feels after Saturday's meal. • Find a figure that elaborates on the information presented in paragraphs 3 and 4.
Identify the elements, strengths, and potential weaknesses of an argument.	• Find two specific pieces of evidence that support the author's claim. • Find the element of the author's argument that you think is weakest or may not hold up to scrutiny.
Compare two or more texts by identifying similarities and differences in content, purpose, and style.	• Read these two tall tales. Find some common elements. • Find information in the first article that's consistent with information in the second article. Find information that conflicts.

Single-Sentence Summaries

Single-Sentence Summaries (Silver & Boutz, 2015) is a tool that capitalizes on the power of both note making and summarizing to make reading more active and reflective. It engages students in note making as they read, and these notes come in the form of summaries that are frequent (typically every paragraph or few paragraphs) and short: each is only one sentence long. This combination of frequency and brevity helps build the summarizing habit in students; over time, it will become second nature for students to stop, process, and jot down the big idea as they read.

It is important to emphasize that students' summary sentences are not to be copied from the text; the summaries should be written in the students' own words and should capture what they believe is most important. So before asking students to use this tool, help build their understanding of what successful summary sentences look and sound like. For example, you can model the process by thinking aloud as you create a single-sentence summary of a paragraph. You might ask students to imagine that the person who wrote the paragraph they have just read is sitting next to them. What would the author likely say is his or her big idea for the paragraph or section? Other ways to teach this process include challenging students to distinguish between stronger and weaker summary sentences, asking students to underline key words that they believe should be included in their summary sentences, and generating a number of single-sentence summaries yourself and having students select (and justify) the one that they believe best summarizes the text. To further acclimate students to using this comprehension-enhancing technique, consider formatting readings to include writing space on the right-hand side for students to summarize each paragraph.

Reading Stances

Sometimes, in our efforts to make sure students walk away with a factual understanding of the texts they read, we lose sight of the fact that reading for understanding is a multifaceted process. What's more, an overemphasis on factual or literal comprehension can come at the expense of student engagement: great motivational power resides in nurturing the reactions and responses students develop while reading. Reading Stances (based on the work of Langer [1994]) is an approach that honors the true dynamism of reading for understanding by inviting students to take a variety of "stances" as they interact with and respond to texts. Through these stances, students build deep and personal meaning. Here is a summary of the four Reading Stances:

- *Literal Stance:* Readers form an initial impression of the text. As they read the words, they are focusing on the literal: *What is this about? What is the topic or gist of the selection? What are the key facts?*

- *Interpretive Stance:* Students develop interpretations of the text, seeking deeper meaning about its embedded concepts and themes. They read "between the lines" to interpret, make inferences, and draw conclusions: *What can I infer or conclude from this text? What is the meaning of _____? What is the implicit theme or message? What meaning lies "between the lines"?*

- *Personal Stance:* Readers connect their personal experiences with the selection. They read "beyond the lines" to explore what the text means to them and how it relates to their lives: *How is this like something from my own experiences? How do I relate to this topic? What does it say to me?*

- *Critical Stance:* Students read analytically and critically. They question the author and the text evaluatively. When reading fiction, they might ask, *How effectively did the author convey the themes, characters, and storyline?* When reading nonfiction, they might ask, *How useful was this information? To what extent is this account accurate, complete, and unbiased?*

To help students understand the stances' purpose and value, introduce the four stances explicitly. Model (e.g., through think-alouds) how you use each stance to explore meaning and respond to the text. Reinforce the way reading comprehension continues to develop *after* reading by using the stances to create post-reading questions that challenge students to summarize important information, think about the text in a variety of ways, express their ideas, and deepen their textual understanding. Figure 5.3 presents sample questions in all four stances for fiction and nonfiction. Note that these same questions can be applied to films, television shows, theater events, political speeches, and other "texts."

FIGURE 5.3

Four Reading Stances with Sample Questions for Fiction and Nonfiction

STANCES	FICTION	NONFICTION
Literal	• What is this [novel, story, poem, etc.] about? • Where is the setting? • When did this piece take place? • Who are the major and minor characters? • What is the situation or problem? • What are the most important events?	• What is the topic or the gist of this [book, article, essay, blog post, etc.]? • What are the key facts? • What is the most important information conveyed? • What did you learn from this?
Interpretive	• What is the meaning of _____? • What is the implicit theme or message? • What is the significance of [the title, an event, a quote, the author's use of figurative language, etc.]? • How would you describe the mood? • What traits do the characters exhibit?	• What is the meaning of _____? • What conclusions can you draw from this text? • What is the [attitude, philosophy, political position, etc.] of the author? • How does this piece compare to [one or more related works]?
Personal	• How is this like something from your life? • How do you relate to this theme? • What did this make you think or feel? • What would you have done if you were the character? • What questions would you like to ask the author/character(s)?	• What did this make you think? • Do you agree with the author? • Are you convinced? Persuaded? • How did it influence your thinking? • What additional information is needed? • What questions would you like to ask the author?
Critical	• What are the greatest strengths of this piece? The greatest weaknesses? • Imagine you are a literary critic. How effectively did the author convey the theme? Describe the setting? Develop the characters? Establish the mood? Unfold the plot? Build to a climax? • How effectively did the author use [flashbacks, irony, symbolism, etc.]? • Would you recommend this to others?	• What are the greatest strengths of this piece? The greatest weaknesses? • How clear was this piece? How accurate? How complete? How unbiased? • How well does the organizational structure work? • How effectively did the author achieve his or her purpose (e.g., to inform or to persuade)?

Let's look at an example from a 1st grade class reading Arnold Lobel's classic story collection *Frog and Toad Are Friends*. The unit was framed as a study of relationships, using the overall essential questions *Who are your true friends? How will you know?* Here are stance questions posed by the teacher:

- *Literal:* Who are the main characters in these stories? Where do the stories take place?
- *Interpretive:* Were there times in the stories when one character was acting like a true friend to the other? Were there times in the stories when one character was not acting like a true friend? Give examples (evidence) from the story to explain and support your answer.
- *Personal:* What kind of person do *you* want as a friend? What is this person like? What are his or her qualities and traits?
- *Critical:* The author included pictures (illustrations). Did these help you understand the stories better? Explain. Should there have been more pictures? If so, of what? Should there have been fewer? If so, which ones would you remove? Why?

Once you have posed stance-related questions, ask students to explain their ideas. Establish the expectation that students should make it a habit to cite evidence from the text to support their responses. Use classroom discussion time to probe student responses and encourage students to elaborate on and explain the textual evidence or reasoning behind their ideas with follow-up questions and prompts, such as *Because . . . ? What led you to that idea/inference/interpretation/conclusion? What evidence from the text shows that? Is there another interpretation? Do you agree with the author?*

Finally, here are two practical suggestions for making the Reading Stances more concrete in the classroom:

1. Create a classroom bulletin board or poster of the four stances and sample questions to remind yourself and your students to use them regularly. For young students, you might use symbols or cartoon characters to represent each stance.

2. Provide a handout or printed bookmark (or have students create their own bookmarks) outlining the four stances and sample questions to encourage students to adopt the four stances when they read.

Reading for Meaning

Reading for Meaning (Silver, Morris, & Klein, 2010; Silver, Strong, & Perini, 2007) is a comprehensive reading-instruction strategy that provides students with the chance to practice and master all three phases of high-level reading (before reading, during reading, and after reading). It works especially well with shorter texts (e.g., articles, poems, primary documents, textbook sections, and novel chapters). Here's how it works.

Before reading, students preview the text and examine a set of statements about the text, which helps them develop a sense of the text's content and key ideas. These statements, designed by the teacher, may be true, false, or open to interpretation. For example, take a look at the middle column labeled "Statements" in Figure 5.4 (p. 66). Before reading the Gettysburg Address in a middle school social studies classroom, students previewed these five statements along with the text itself to help them build a prereading sense of what the text would include.

During reading, students use the statements to actively guide their search for important information. They collect anything they find in the text that either supports or challenges any of the statements. Figure 5.4 shows the textual evidence from the Gettysburg Address that a student collected, recording information that seemed to support particular statements on the left and information that seemed to refute particular statements on the right. Notice that for the first statement, the student collected evidence both for and against the statement, which is a great sign of internal debate and active reading.

After reading, students work in small groups to summarize the key ideas and review the statements, their predictions, and the textual evidence they collected. Groups try to reach consensus on each statement (e.g., "The evidence in the text clearly supports or refutes this statement because . . ."). For any statements that students can't reach consensus on, the group is encouraged to rewrite the statement so that all students can agree that it is either fully supported or fully refuted by the text.

FIGURE 5.4

Reading for Meaning Organizer: Gettysburg Address

Evidence That Supports	Statements	Evidence That Refutes
"We have come to dedicate a portion of that field, as a final resting place for those who here gave their lives that that nation might live."	The primary goal of the speech was to honor the soldiers who had fought and died.	"It is for us the living, rather, to be dedicated here to the unfinished work . . . to the great task remaining before us."
"Now we are engaged in a great civil war, testing whether that nation, or any nation so conceived and so dedicated, can long endure."	Lincoln believed the United States was at a crossroads.	
	Lincoln believed that the outcome of the war had implications only for the U.S.	"The <u>world</u> will little note, nor long remember what we say here, but it can never forget what they did here. . . . shall not perish from the <u>earth</u>."
• "Four score and seven years ago" —past • "Now we are engaged"—present • "Shall not perish from the earth" —future	Lincoln takes the reader on a journey through time.	
"The brave men . . . who struggled here, have consecrated it, far above our poor power to add or detract. The world will . . . never forget what they did here."	Lincoln would agree that actions speak louder than words.	

Summing Up

Ask any teacher about the importance of reading for understanding—of reading texts closely and using textual evidence to develop and support interpretations—and you'll likely receive a universal answer: students' success absolutely depends upon it. To help all students build this essential meaning-making skill, we have paid close attention to how the most successful readers build their understanding through reading. More specifically, we have focused on how proficient readers approach a text (before reading), read actively and with purpose (during reading), and solidify their learning (after reading). The tools in this chapter will help students adopt this proficient-reader approach so that they consistently get more out of the texts they read.

6

Predicting and Hypothesizing

The *What* and *Why* of Predicting and Hypothesizing

Will it sink, or will it float? First graders eagerly strain to see as their teacher places the next object into a tub of water. Before testing each item, students make a new prediction: will it sink or float? The classroom erupts into squeals as students watch various objects bob or drop.

A palpable hush overtakes a room full of 6th graders as their math teacher stands on a big zero on the floor and proceeds to do the moonwalk. "Now that I've embarrassed myself with my '80s dance moves," she says, "your job is to guess what my moonwalk has to do with our upcoming unit." (It turns out to be on negative numbers.)

High school sociology students huddle around the survey data they've collected to test their hypothesis that reducing social media usage leads to lower stress levels in students. They're vigorously debating whether the data supports or refutes their team's hypothesis—or whether more data is needed.

In all these scenarios, learners are making predictions or generating and testing hypotheses. From these scenarios, we can glean the instructional power of these two thinking processes. Both predicting and hypothesizing engage students in the active construction of meaning by asking them to think speculatively and then test the strength and validity of their ideas against results or new evidence.

So, if the process of generating and testing ideas is what predicting and hypothesizing have in common, what's different about them? Let's take a closer look at these two thinking processes.

To *predict* is an attempt to foretell an outcome before it occurs. People make dozens of predictions daily. Based on our prior experiences, some are nearly automatic. For example, when we plan more time for our daily commute during a rainy rush hour, we are predicting that traffic will be heavier and travel time will be longer than during sunny weather or off-peak hours. Some predictions are calculated: as frequent flyers, both authors of this book carefully watch the progression of the TSA lines at airports and try to avoid the ones with baby strollers and less-frequent travelers who do not know the drill. A prediction can also be nothing more than a wild guess, as when a novice gambler takes on a roulette wheel in Las Vegas. More fateful predictions are generated in the face of uncertainty, as when we must decide on a life-changing course of action, such as taking a spouse or accepting a new job. In making decisions like these, we tend to use our own experiences and whatever evidence we can find to predict the consequences of our decisions (e.g., that the marriage will be fulfilling or that the new job will offer an exciting challenge, better pay, and greater satisfaction).

When it comes to the importance of prediction in school and in life, few have said it more clearly than Judy Willis, a board-certified neurologist who left medicine after more than 20 years to become a teacher. According to Willis,

> Through observations, experiences, and feedback, the brain increasingly learns about the world and can make progressively more accurate predictions about what will come next and how to respond to new information, problems, or choices. This ability for prediction, guided by pattern recognition, is a foundation for successful literacy, numeracy, test taking, appropriate social-emotional behavior, and understanding. Successful prediction is one of the brain's best problem-solving strategies. (McTighe & Willis, 2019, p. 9)

What about hypothesizing? Although the terms *hypothesis* and *prediction* are often used interchangeably—likely because hypotheses enable us to make predictions—they're not the same thing. A hypothesis is a proposed explanation, not a prediction. More specifically, it's "usually a tentative, testable . . . *explanation* for *why* something is the way it is, or happens the way it does" (Flammer, Beard, Nelson, & Nickels, n.d.). Because hypotheses are tentative, they need to be investigated and tested. And it's the results of those tests and investigations that serve to determine the hypotheses' validity. (*Do these results support my hypothesis? Or disprove it?*)

Another common misconception about hypothesizing is that it's "just for scientists." Although people in different fields may define hypothesizing slightly differently, generate different types of hypotheses, and use different methods to test them—a historian, for example, might test a hypothesis by examining primary documents, a scientist might conduct an experiment, and an archaeologist might look for artifacts—the basic process of generating and testing possible explanations is used across virtually all fields and disciplines and by people of all ages.

When historians make educated guesses about why something happened the way it did and conduct research to test their ideas, they're generating and testing hypotheses. When an advertising executive guesses why an ad campaign is failing and begins investigating those possibilities, that executive is generating and testing hypotheses. When a curious child tries to isolate the reason why one toy car always beats the others down a ramp, that child is generating and testing hypotheses. Thus, the process of generating and testing explanations is both universally used and universally valuable. This reality underscores the importance of teaching hypothesizing not just in upper-level science classes but also in all content areas and grade levels.

When teachers engage students in hypothesizing by presenting them with information, observations, or phenomena that spark curiosity and beg an explanation, they reap many benefits. Classroom hypothesizing promotes students' natural curiosity, prompting learners to wonder why. It promotes the kind of active thinking and engagement that leads to deep understanding. It develops valuable and transferable thinking skills. And it's an effective strategy for boosting achievement (Dean et al., 2012).

Clearly, both predicting and hypothesizing are important skills in the classroom and beyond. But not all predictions and hypotheses are created equal. Reasoned predictions and sound hypotheses (as opposed to wild guesses and thoughtless explanations) are informed by pattern recognition and causal reasoning. By noting *patterns* based on prior experiences or accumulated data, we can extrapolate to make a prediction about what may happen in the future or venture a theory about the *cause* of an event or a phenomenon.

The *How* of Predicting and Hypothesizing

Both predicting and hypothesizing can be productively applied at every grade level and in all subjects. And if teachers work to engage learners in these related thinking skills, we *predict* the following benefits:

- *Increased attention, focus, and curiosity at the start of instruction.* Having learners venture a prediction or generate a hypothesis before a lesson begins creates intrigue, helps students tease out their prior knowledge, and gets their minds "primed" for new learning. It also serves as a powerful pre-assessment technique (e.g., by illuminating student misconceptions).

- *More active engagement and deeper thinking throughout the instructional process.* By enlisting the skills of predicting and hypothesizing during instruction, teachers can promote pattern recognition and causal reasoning, encourage students to develop and evaluate their own ideas, stimulate students to pursue further research and investigation, and foster the kind of meaning making that leads to deep understanding.

To help you achieve these benefits, we present four instructional tools:

1. **Prediction- and Hypothesis-Based Hooks** offers a variety of ways to capture student attention, stimulate curiosity, and set up new learning at the outset of lessons and units.

2. **Inductive Learning** engages students in pattern recognition and prediction by challenging them to analyze specific information, look for commonalities, and make informed predictions about the learning to come.

3. **Mystery** challenges students to piece together clues and to use those clues to develop and support sound hypotheses.

4. **If-Then** lays out a simple process for generating hypotheses, predicting outcomes, and testing ideas.

Prediction- and Hypothesis-Based Hooks

A good hook at the beginning of a lesson will stimulate curiosity, encourage students to review their prior knowledge, and get students to start constructing meaning—all before the lesson begins. While there are many ways to design good hooks, few are more effective than those that engage students in making predictions or generating tentative hypotheses, which they can then test as they learn more during the lesson or unit. The following are a few of our favorite prediction- and hypothesis-based techniques for hooking students' interest.

What If? "What if?" questions posed at the outset of a lesson invite students to use existing knowledge to make predictions or hypotheses that help frame the learning to come. Following are some examples:

- What if there were no plants? Make some predictions about how your life would be different.
- What if you traveled 200 years into the future and discovered that the United States was no longer the world's greatest power? Generate some hypotheses about what caused this change. (This was used to introduce a lesson on the causes of the fall of Rome.)
- What if negative numbers didn't exist?
- What if there were no rules or laws to influence our behavior? (This was used to introduce the novel *Lord of the Flies*.)
- What if the framers of the U.S. Constitution had written it to truly ensure equal rights for all Americans?
- What if schools put a greater emphasis on promoting creativity?

Yes, But Why? This questioning technique invites hypothesizing by getting students to think deeply about the reasons behind important aspects of the content that are usually taken for granted or that students tend to oversimplify. For example, if you ask students why liquid comes up through a straw, they will typically answer that sucking on the straw simply makes the liquid come up. (The "yes, but why?" of it is that sucking on the straw creates less air pressure on the liquid inside the straw than outside, resulting in an imbalance that causes more liquid to be forced into the straw.) Yes,

But Why? can be used to set up inquiries into topics that students are about to begin exploring. Here are a few examples:

- Yes, some animals hibernate and others don't. But why?
- Yes, dividing by zero is impossible. But why?
- Yes, *The Catcher in the Rye* is banned in many schools. But why?
- Yes, songs written in minor keys often sound sad. But why?

Questions That Puzzle; Data That Teases. Starting a lesson with a puzzling question or with data that is surprising, intriguing, or counterintuitive is a natural way to raise curiosity and engage students in predicting or hypothesizing. Here are some examples:

- A middle school science teacher shows students a picture of a fossil of a fern plant, along with a map showing the locations on all the continents where similar fossils have been found. Then the teacher poses this question: "How can this data be used to support the claim that Earth's continents were once one giant supercontinent?"
- A U.S. history teacher asks students to generate some explanations as to why public support for U.S. involvement in Vietnam fell from nearly 70 percent to under 40 percent in just two years.
- When a 5th grade teacher asks students to predict what happens to the temperature as you go higher in the Earth's atmosphere, most predict that the temperature steadily increases ("because you're moving closer to the sun"). Others who have experienced that it gets cold up in the mountains predict the opposite—that is, that temperatures get increasingly lower at higher altitudes. Thus, they're all puzzled when their teacher presents a data chart (see Figure 6.1) showing that there's neither a steady increase nor a steady decrease in temperature as you rise higher in the Earth's atmosphere. Before showing a video that explains why these variations occur, the teacher asks students to use what they've learned about the layers of the Earth's atmosphere to generate some possible hypotheses.
- A primary teacher who is beginning a unit on bedtime uses the following questions to hook students' interest and get them thinking speculatively: "Why do we even need bedtimes? What might happen if kids were allowed to stay up as late as they wanted?"

FIGURE 6.1

Temperatures in the Atmospheric Layers

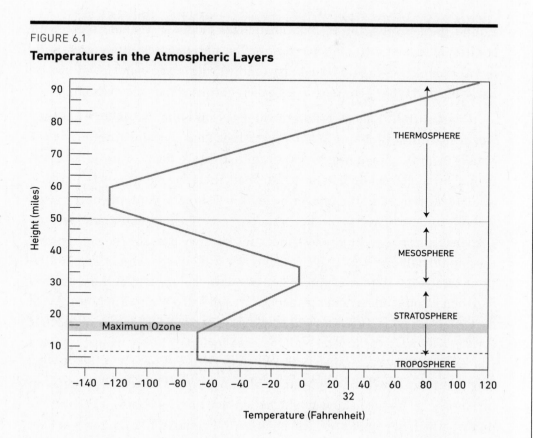

Discrepant Events. Unexpected outcomes and anomalous events pique curiosity because they challenge our understanding of the world and of how things work. Better yet, from an instructional standpoint, they compel students to generate hypotheses about what is happening and why. For example, a middle school science teacher begins an inquiry with this unexpected phenomenon: when placing two full cans of soda into a container of water, one can sinks and the other floats, even though both cans have the same volume of liquid inside. Students generate and share hypotheses about why the two cans behave differently, which the teacher records on the board. Students' task for the remainder of the lesson is to test the various hypotheses and to figure out what is causing the different results. (The main cause is sugar. One can contains regular soda and the other contains sugar-free soda, which affects the density—but not the volume—of each can.) To extend the learning, the teacher challenges students to experiment with additional variables that might cause different outcomes. Students experiment with factors including salinity (adding salt to the water), water temperature, and type of container (e.g., glass bottles versus metal cans).

Crystal Ball. This technique challenges students to predict what they will be learning by looking into a "crystal ball" that contains specific facts or details from the upcoming lesson or unit. To start, draw or project a crystal ball on the board. Inside the crystal ball, include a set of words, phrases, or pictures related to the upcoming lesson. Using the contents of the crystal ball, students have to predict what the lesson will be about. To increase suspense and make the process more interactive, present the contents of the crystal ball one item at a time, and ask students to refine their predictions after each item presented. For example, before beginning a unit on weather, a 2nd grade teacher projects a crystal ball on the whiteboard. With each click, a new picture that will help students predict the topic of the unit is revealed inside the crystal ball. Pictures include a heavy winter jacket, a tree with no leaves, an umbrella, the sun, and a thermometer. A high school English teacher presents eight lines from Act II of *Macbeth* that come up one by one on her projected crystal ball. Based on these lines, students predict what will happen in the act. Then, as they read Act II, students collect evidence to support or refute their predictions.

Inductive Learning

One way to enhance students' predictive power is to teach them how to think inductively. When students are able to analyze bits of information and identify patterns within them, their ability to make sound, well-reasoned predictions grows in turn. Inductive Learning is a teaching strategy based on the pioneering work of Hilda Taba (Taba, Durkin, Fraenkel, & McNaughton, 1971). It's designed to help students learn to use the power of induction to discover big ideas and make informed predictions. A great benefit of this tool is that it challenges students to construct the conceptual overview of whatever they're learning on their own—a bold instructional move that can have a dramatic effect on student understanding. To use Inductive Learning in your classroom, follow these steps:

1. Identify the big ideas in the content you are about to present or teach (e.g., a reading, lesson, or unit).

2. Select 15–40 specific terms or phrases that relate to your big ideas. Aim for a mix of familiar and unfamiliar terms.

3. Distribute the terms to students. Allow students to look up any unfamiliar terms.

4. Place students in small groups and ask them to analyze the terms and explore different ways the information can be grouped. If students are new to the process, model the process using a highly relatable topic (e.g., items in a grocery store).

5. Challenge students to organize all the terms into groups. (Note that students can put the same term into multiple groups.) For each group that students create, they must devise a descriptive label that captures the big idea of the grouping. *Tip:* encourage students to think beyond the obvious— to look for interesting relationships and ways to combine their initial groups into larger, more inclusive groups.

6. Ask students to review their groups and labels and use them to make predictions about the learning to come.

7. As the learning progresses, have students collect evidence that supports or refutes each prediction. Students should refine their predictions in light of new learning.

A scenario from *The Core Six* (Silver, Dewing, & Perini, 2012) showed a middle school teacher using Inductive Learning to design a lesson on the Mississippian Indians that allowed students to construct their own conceptual understanding of the content. She began by presenting students with 25 specific terms that supported the big ideas of the lesson. For instance, to help students discover the importance of agriculture to the Mississippian Indians, she included a mix of common words like *squash* and *beans* along with new academic terms like *crop rotation* and *digging sticks*. Working in small teams, students analyzed all 25 terms, looked up new terms, and grouped common terms together based on common characteristics. For each group that students created, they devised a descriptive label that clarified what the items in the group had in common. One student team created the set of groups and labels shown in Figure 6.2.

FIGURE 6.2

A Student Team's Groups and Labels: Mississippian Indians

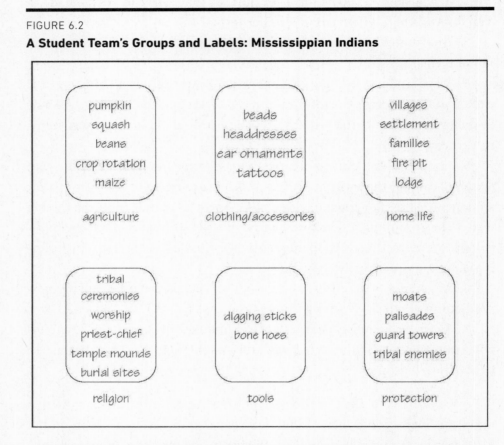

Source: From *The Core Six: Essential Strategies for Achieving Excellence with the Common Core* (p. 30), by H. F. Silver, R. T. Dewing, and M. J. Perini, 2012, Alexandria, VA: ASCD. © 2012 ASCD.

Once students developed their big-idea groups, their teacher challenged them to use those groups to make three predictions about the Mississippian Indians. The student team that created the labeled groups shown in Figure 6.2 made the following three predictions:

1. Mississippian Indians were farmers.

2. They had more elaborate clothes than earlier pre-colonial people we learned about.

3. They believed in an afterlife.

As students continued to learn about the Mississippian Indians, they collected evidence that confirmed or challenged their predictions and refined their thinking based on new learning.

Inductive Learning is a great way to help students make meaning and generate predictions before a lesson or unit begins, as shown in the preceding example. It is also a highly versatile strategy that can be used in other ways, including the following:

- *To review content already learned.* Give students the terms they have already learned near the end of the unit, and challenge them to create a conceptual map that reveals their understanding of the big ideas in the unit and the details that support each big idea.

- *To develop students' classification skills.* For example, a primary-grade teacher organized a field trip around the school for students to search for all the organisms or signs of organisms they could find. Back in the classroom, students compiled all their findings and worked with their teacher to develop a classification system for the various organisms they identified.

- *To help students recognize patterns in nonlinguistic information.* Instead of providing terms for students to group and label, try using paintings in an art class, equations in a math class, pictures of various biomes in a science class, and so on.

- *To build students' prewriting planning skills.* Teach students how to generate ideas before writing, organize their ideas into groups, and make each group the basis of a paragraph. Challenge students to create a topic sentence for each paragraph that tells what the paragraph will be about and to use the ideas they collected as supporting details within each paragraph.

Mystery

Mystery (Silver et al., 2007) makes the process of generating and testing hypotheses one that students *want* to engage in by presenting them with content-related "mysteries" and challenging them to develop and test possible explanations using teacher-provided "clues." Clues can take any format (e.g., data tables, images, sentence strips), and the phenomena students investigate can come from any content area. A science teacher, for example, might challenge students to solve the mystery of why the dinosaurs disappeared, whereas an art teacher might challenge students to figure out why Impressionism—one of the most celebrated artistic movements in history—was hated by art critics at the time.

The overall structure and procedures for a Mystery lesson are similar to those of an Inductive Learning lesson: students analyze bits of information, organize related bits into groups, and give those groups descriptive labels. In a Mystery lesson, however, students analyze and group *clues* rather than *terms* and generate *hypotheses* rather than *predictions*. Teachers also initiate a Mystery lesson differently—specifically, by framing an event, a phenomenon, or a concept that they want students to understand as a mystery.

For example, a social studies teacher who wanted students to understand the factors that triggered the Age of Exploration motivated students to discover those factors for themselves by presenting this mystery: "For much of European history, no real efforts were made to explore the world by sea. Why, all of a sudden, was there an 'exploration explosion' in the 15th century?"

After organizing students into teams and distributing the "clues" he had developed (slips of paper containing information about the various factors that contributed to the exploration explosion), the teacher instructed students to group related clues together and use those groupings to generate tentative hypotheses for "why the time was right" in the 15th century. Figure 6.3 shows a clue group that one team generated, along with the hypothesis it led students to develop.

Other clue groups students created led to hypotheses that additional factors—including the desire to expand Christianity, competition among nations, and the loss of trade routes by land—also contributed to the exploration explosion. After sharing their hypotheses and the "clue evidence" that supported them as a class, students used a textbook passage on the Age of Exploration to check and revise their hypotheses.

FIGURE 6.3

A Student Team's Clue Group and Hypothesis

Clue 4: The science of mapmaking had become sophisticated and increasingly accurate by Columbus's time.

Clue 9: Inventions like the astrolabe and mariner's compass made longer and more difficult trips possible.

Clue 20: New ships called caravels were faster and easier to navigate than any ship before.

We hypothesize that the time was right for exploration in the 15th century because advances in technology and mapmaking made farther, safer trips possible.

Source: From Tools for Classroom Instruction That Works: Ready-to-Use Techniques for Increasing Student Achievement *(p. 213), by H. F. Silver, C. Abla, A. L. Boutz, and M. J. Perini, 2018, Franklin Lakes, NJ: Silver Strong & Associates/Thoughtful Education Press and McREL International. © 2018 Silver Strong & Associates. Used with permission.*

If-Then

The process of generating and testing hypotheses is one of the most potent ways in which experts in various fields make meaning and advance ideas. But many students equate the term *hypothesis* with something akin to guessing. If-Then clarifies what a hypothesis actually is and outlines a simple process for generating and testing hypotheses. This tool also folds in the skill of predicting, as students forecast the results that their hypotheses will lead to before testing them.

To use If-Then in the classroom, follow these steps:

1. Focus students' attention on a phenomenon that calls for an explanation. (The phenomenon can be one that students observe directly or one that others have observed or reported on—for example, the recent rise in food allergies.) Then pose a question that asks students to generate possible and plausible explanations for that phenomenon.

Example: After challenging students to increase profits at the school snack stand, a high school business teacher called students' attention to the fact that the burger with the lowest profit margin (the Crandale Cheeseburger) was outselling the more profitable burgers on the menu—and challenged students to generate possible explanations why.

2. Invite students to develop and then share proposed explanations with the class. Teach students that these proposed explanations are called *hypotheses*.

Example: Hypothesis #1: The Crandale Cheeseburger is outselling the other burgers because it is the first burger listed on the menu.

Hypothesis #2: The Crandale Cheeseburger is outselling the other burgers because it has the lowest price.

Hypothesis #3: The Crandale Cheeseburger is outselling the other burgers because it is the only burger with a color photo.

3. Generate (or challenge students to generate) one or more ways to test their hypotheses. Remind students that testing a hypothesis can be done in different ways, including carrying out experiments, making observations, performing calculations, or analyzing existing data.

Example: Students might propose testing the various hypotheses they generated by swapping the placement of the burgers on the menu, pricing all the burgers the same, or adding photos of the other burgers.

4. If necessary, help students flesh out and improve the design of their proposed experiments or tests.

5. Ask students to predict what the outcomes of their proposed tests or experiments would be if their hypotheses are correct. Predictions should be framed using an If-Then format, as shown below.

If it's true that <u>including a color picture of an item increases its sales</u>,
                                (hypothesis)
then we would expect that <u>adding pictures of the higher-profit burgers</u>
                                (test)
would lead to <u>an increase in the sales of the higher-profit burgers</u>.
                                (predicted outcome)

6. Have students conduct their proposed tests or experiments and record the results. If students' proposed experiments can't be carried out owing to limitations in resources, skill level, or any other factor, provide students with sample data that they can analyze and use to complete Step 7.

7. Ask students whether the predictions they made in Step 5 were correct. If so, students should conclude that their experimental data supports their hypotheses. If not, students should either revise their existing hypotheses to account for the results or generate entirely new hypotheses.

Summing Up

Predicting and hypothesizing are fundamental human thinking skills linked to biological survival. By employing the tools presented in this chapter, teachers invite students to make and defend predictions or generate and test hypotheses. In so doing, they can spark interest while engaging concomitant skills of observation, causal reasoning, inductive thinking, pattern analysis, and justification. Applying these valuable thinking skills leads to deeper learning and helps make the content come alive in the classroom.

7

Visualizing and Graphic Representation

The *What* and *Why* of Visualizing and Graphic Representation

Retrieve a memory from high school.

No, really. Please—we're asking nicely.

Close your eyes if it helps. It's important. A bet rides on it.

So do you have a memory? Good, now let's see if we won our bet.

We're not gamblers, but this is one bet we are willing to make: we bet that the memory you retrieved came in the form of an image. This is a high-odds bet because humans understand and retain important information by forming mental models that capture the gist of that information. That's why visualizing is so powerful in the classroom: it capitalizes on what the brain does uncannily well—and how the brain makes meaning. Citing the work of brain researcher John Medina (2008), the authors of *Classroom Instruction That Works* explain that nonlinguistic strategies "are powerful because they tap into students' natural tendency for visual image processing, which helps them construct meaning of relevant content and skills and have a better capacity to recall it later" (Dean et al., 2012, p. 64). It should come as little wonder, then, that a synthesis of research studies associated with the use of nonlinguistic representation in the classroom found a significant and positive effect on student achievement (Beesley & Apthorp, 2010; Dean et al., 2012).

One reason visualizing improves students' meaning-making capacity has to do with something called *dual coding* (Paivio, 1990). The best way to

82

describe dual coding is to trot out the old maxim "Two are better than one," but with this important addition: ". . . especially when the two work as one." Dual coding works because it takes advantage of two distinct channels that the brain uses for processing information: a visual channel and a verbal or linguistic channel. Working together, each increases the power of the other, making dual coding a highly effective way to enhance students' understanding and retention of what they learn.

More generally, visualizing facilitates meaning making because the very act of converting information into a visual form is one of transformation, which requires active processing on the learner's part. And keep in mind that visualizing is more than pictures and symbols. Graphic organizers offer another means of nonlinguistic representation that can greatly enhance learning. In this chapter, we explore the use of visualization through images and image making as well as graphic organizers that support nonlinguistic representation.

The *How* of Visualizing and Graphic Representation

If visualizing is so powerful, what should teachers do about it? What are some effective ways to use it to enhance students' meaning-making capacities? How can teachers incorporate visualization and graphic representation into everyday instruction without reinventing their current practice? To help answer these questions, we present the following five instructional tools. Deliberate use of these tools in your classroom will enable you and your students to harness the meaning-making power of visualization and graphic representation.

1. **Don't Just Say It; Display It** serves as a simple reminder of the impact well-chosen images can have on student understanding, especially when those images are explained and discussed during classroom presentations and conversations.

2. **Split Screen** helps you integrate dual coding seamlessly into classroom presentations and learning experiences by inviting students to process new learning through images and words.

3. **Mind's Eye** enhances reading comprehension by teaching students how to create mental images before reading and then use those images to engage deeply with the text.

4. **Visualizing Vocabulary** promotes deep understanding of key concepts and vocabulary terms by challenging students to transform their knowledge into symbols or icons and then explain how those symbols represent essential information about the concept.

5. **Graphic Organizers** show how information can be visually arranged, helping students to see the big picture of what they're learning—and the relationships between important chunks of content.

Don't Just Say It; Display It

Everyone knows the saying about a picture being worth a thousand words, including brain researchers. Indeed, as John Medina (2008) points out, "Put simply, the more visual the input becomes, the more likely it is to be recognized—and recalled" (p. 233). Don't Just Say It; Display It encourages teachers to take the old saying to heart by incorporating relevant images into their classroom presentations and explaining how the chosen images relate to the content under investigation. For example, if you are teaching the concept of *mutualism* (when two organisms of different species work together, with each benefiting from the relationship), you can help students concretize their understanding by showing and explaining a picture like the one in Figure 7.1. The picture shows the abstract concept of mutualism at work: the bird gets food off the rhino's hide, the rhino gets pest control—and the students get a serious understanding boost. This understanding will become even deeper if you ask students to explain why the image is a good representation of mutualism rather than providing the explanation yourself.

Be on the lookout for images that you can incorporate into your classroom presentations to illustrate key concepts you want learners to understand. Or invite students to create the images on their own, as described in the following section.

Split Screen

You can increase the benefits of visualization by giving students the responsibility to develop their own images and explain how those images represent their understanding. Split Screen (Silver et al., 2018) builds this

FIGURE 7.1

A Visualization of Mutualism

important skill in students, teaching them how to process and encode new learning first through images, then through language. It is especially helpful in making the content of classroom lectures and presentations vivid and meaningful for students.

To use the Split Screen tool in your classroom, follow these basic steps:

1. Organize the information you will be presenting into meaningful chunks. For example, a presentation on the Great Wall of China might be broken up into these four chunks: (1) Who built it? (2) How was it built? (3) Why was it built? (4) What's so amazing about it?

2. Present a single chunk of content. Stop and instruct students to think about the most important ideas and how they might represent them visually. Give students a minute or two to draw their representations on a Split Screen organizer (see Figure 7.2, p. 86).

FIGURE 7.2

A 2nd Grader's Split Screen Notes: Snakeskin

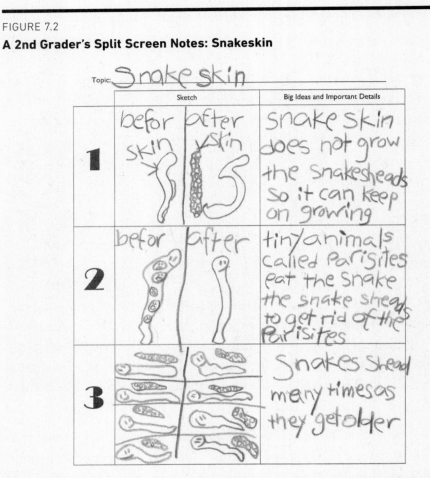

Source: From *Tools for Classroom Instruction That Works: Ready-to-Use Techniques for Increasing Student Achievement* (p. 136), by H. F. Silver, C. Abla, A. L. Boutz, and M. J. Perini, 2018, Franklin Lakes, NJ: Silver Strong & Associates/Thoughtful Education Press and McREL International. © 2018 Silver Strong & Associates. Used with permission.

3. After students have completed their drawings, allow them to meet in pairs or small groups to compare images, guess what one another's images represent, and discuss the big ideas that they were trying to capture in their sketches.

4. Ask students to explain in the right-hand column of the organizer how their image summarizes the big ideas and details of the content presented.

5. Repeat steps 2–4 until all the chunks of information have been presented and processed.

When introducing this technique, take the time to teach students how to make notes using images rather than words. Model how you would capture the big ideas of a particular chunk of content in visual form. What's critically important is that students understand the true goal of the image making—not to draw every detail, but to draw simple images that capture important ideas.

Figure 7.2 shows a 2nd grader's Split Screen notes. Notice how the student drew the big ideas about how and why snakes shed their skin and then explained each image on the right. Clearly, this student understands the important information deeply.

Mind's Eye

The ability to construct mental pictures while reading has a dramatic and positive effect on reading comprehension (Wilhelm, 2012). Mind's Eye (Silver et al., 2018; adapted from the work of Brownlie & Silver [1995] and Pressley [1979]) is a tool that teaches students how to create mental pictures before reading and then use those images to help them make meaning during the reading process. It is also a great engagement booster, as it can increase students' interest in the texts they read and create a driving purpose for reading. Mind's Eye works best with short- to medium-length works of fiction (e.g., short stories, fables, novel chapters) and plot-driven nonfiction (e.g., excerpts from a biography, an autobiography, or a memoir).

Prior to having students read, the teacher selects 10–20 keywords or phrases from the text. The chosen words and phrases should contain visual or other sensory information that will help students picture the text in their mind. The words should also reveal information about key aspects of the text (e.g., setting-related words and phrases like *tropical island, sailing ship,* and *coconuts;* character-related words and phrases like *handsomely dressed, haughty,* and *boastful;* and action-related words and phrases like *shrieked, cheated,* and *ran for her life*). The teacher reads each word or phrase aloud slowly, adding emphasis, sound effects, or emotions when appropriate. Meanwhile, the students close their eyes and try to picture the story in their minds. With each word, students adjust their mental images. After students have created a kind of mental "movie" of the text based on the selected words, they are invited to choose one or more activities from the following list:

1. Draw a scene from their mental movie.
2. Generate questions they have about the story.
3. Make predictions about the story.
4. Describe feelings or personal connections that their images evoked.

For example, before having her 3rd graders read Barbara Cooney's classic children's book *Miss Rumphius*, a teacher reads aloud a set of keywords from the text to students. Students use these words to create their mental movies and then complete all four Mind's Eye activities. One student's work is shown in Figure 7.3.

Now primed for active reading, the students approach the text with purpose: looking for answers to their questions, assessing the accuracy of their pictures and predictions, and considering how their feelings about the story have changed.

FIGURE 7.3

A Student's Mind's Eye Organizer: *Miss Rumphius*

KEY WORDS: grandfather, artist, stories, library, books, sailing ship, faraway places, tropical islands, beaches, coconuts, mountains, jungles, lions, house by the sea, friends, crazy, seeds, flowers, beautiful, happy

Mind's Eye Organizer

Name of text: Miss Rumphius	Author: Barbara Cooney
PICTURE	**FEELINGS or PERSONAL CONNECTIONS** I feel peaceful. There are many words that make me feel peaceful like beaches, library, happy, and beautiful.
QUESTIONS Did some people believe that Miss Rumphius was crazy? Why did they think that?	**PREDICTIONS** I think Miss Rumphius will go sailing and see faraway places like tropical islands and jungles. Or maybe she will imagine these places by reading about them in the library.

Source: From *Tools for Classroom Instruction That Works: Ready-to-Use Techniques for Increasing Student Achievement* (p. 131), by H. F. Silver, C. Abla, A. L. Boutz, and M. J. Perini, 2018, Franklin Lakes, NJ: Silver Strong & Associates/ Thoughtful Education Press and McREL International. © 2018 Silver Strong & Associates. Used with permission.

Visualizing Vocabulary

Research on vocabulary acquisition stresses the importance of teaching vocabulary as concepts rather than as words to be memorized (Marzano, 2009). Such an approach can be enhanced through visualization and, more specifically, by challenging students to create images that represent their conceptual understanding of important vocabulary terms. What are the critical attributes of the term in question? How can students best represent one or more of its defining attributes? Visualizing Vocabulary (Silver et al., 2018) engages students in a productive struggle when learning concepts and vocabulary terms—a struggle to transform their understanding into images or symbols and then explain why their images are good representations of the terms they're learning. The tool also makes learning personal, because the images students generate represent their own understanding rather than what the textbook or teacher tells them. Establishing this kind of personal meaning making can be especially beneficial when students are learning new vocabulary terms (Dean et al., 2012). For example, an elementary student used this tool to visualize and explain his very own understanding of the term *freedom* (see Figure 7.4).

FIGURE 7.4

An Elementary Student Visualizes and Explains *Freedom*

Freedom is the right to do what you want.

Sketch:

Explanation:

This bird has freedom. It is not in the cage. It is flying in the sky.

Source: From *Word Works: Cracking Vocabulary's CODE* (2nd Edition) (p. 39), by Thoughtful Education Press, 2008, Franklin Lakes, NJ: Author. © 2008 Thoughtful Education Press. Used with permission.

You can use Visualizing Vocabulary to place special attention on a small number of critical concepts, or you can use it more systematically, as a way to help students make meaning of multiple academic terms they encounter within a unit. To use the tool in coordination with the academic vocabulary of an entire unit, follow these steps:

1. Identify the most important concepts and terms in the unit. Focus your attention on the critical concepts and academic terms rather than every new term.

2. Provide, or have students create, a five-column glossary (see Figure 7.5). Introduce the terms and allow students to write down each term and its textbook or dictionary definition in their glossaries.

3. As students learn more about each term, encourage them to rewrite the definition in their own words.

4. Tell students that once they feel they have a solid understanding of the term, they should create an image or a symbol that represents the term and explain why their image is a good representation of the term.

5. Allow students to share their images and explanations in small groups or as a class, and give students the chance to add to or refine their definitions and images if they choose.

6. Encourage students to use their glossaries as a study guide.

FIGURE 7.5

A Student's Visualizing Vocabulary Glossary: Intro to Film (Excerpt)

Term	Textbook Definition	My Definition	Image/Symbol/Icon	Explanation
Narrative	A cinematic structure in which content is selected and arranged in a sequence.	The story or plot of a movie		I drew a book on a screen to show that the movie is telling a story called a narrative.
Realism	An interest or concern for the actual or real	A style of filmmaking that focuses on real life and how people really live.		I drew a regular person outside a regular house. The mirror is reflecting them because realism reflects or shows real life.

Finally, keep in mind that forms of nonlinguistic representation other than visualization can also be used to deepen understanding of key vocabulary. As education author and consultant Bj Stone (2016) reminds us, when students use multiple nonlinguistic ways to represent terms,

> the probability of deeper understanding and longer retention increases. For example, students learning the vocabulary word *defenestrate*, which means to throw something out the window, might kinesthetically demonstrate the word, followed by sketching what it looks like to defenestrate. Ultimately, students should be given time to create a mental picture of how they look at defenestrating an object. (para. 7)

Graphic Organizers

Like image-rich instruction, graphic organizers take advantage of the natural learning boost that visualization offers. But rather than enhancing understanding via symbols, icons, or pictures, a graphic organizer works more like a map of the content, giving students a visual, holistic representation of facts, concepts, and their relationships within an organized frame. Graphic organizers can take a wide variety of forms, and they are highly versatile. They can be used to

- Represent abstract information in a more concrete form.
- Depict relationships among facts and concepts.
- Relate new information to prior knowledge.
- Focus teaching and learning on the most important ideas.
- Generate ideas and organize thoughts for speaking, writing, and multimedia presentations.

The use of graphic organizers enhances meaning making and promotes deep understanding of critical content—especially when reinforced through questioning and summarizing. In this section, we take a closer look at four different types of graphic organizers: advance organizers, story maps, concept maps, and student-generated visual organizers. (A fifth type of graphic organizing technique known as webbing is discussed in Chapter 3.)

Advance organizers present learners with a basic framework showing the main content chunks that students will be learning. Students use the organizer to integrate new information into the larger framework and build their understanding of the content. Here's an example to drive home the power of an advance organizer. Think back to how you learned about the U.S. Constitution. What do you remember? What if your history teacher began your class's unit on the Constitution by showing you the simple organizer in Figure 7.6?

FIGURE 7.6

Advance Organizer Showing Parts of the U.S. Constitution

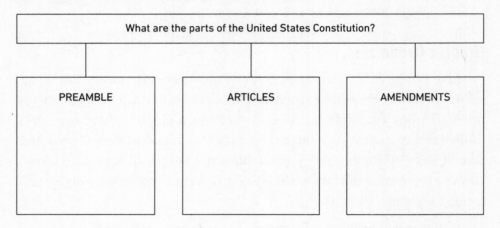

Now imagine that this organizer guided your learning before, during, and after instruction, so that . . .

• Before any input, the teacher presented this advance organizer to help you see how the information you were about to learn was structured.

• During instruction, your teacher stopped after each chunk of information, giving you the chance to collect information in the appropriate space, prompting you to review your notes and revise them for accuracy or new insights, and posing thoughtful questions about each chunk to help you process the new learning deeply.

• After instruction, your teacher asked you to review what you learned and summarize it in your own words.

This way of presenting content in clear chunks, coupled with ongoing formative assessment to guide the meaning-making process, can have a dramatic effect on student understanding (Schmoker, 2018). An important part of this process lies in matching the organizer you use to the specifics of the content. For example, if students will be learning about the key similarities and differences between insects and spiders, you would select a comparison organizer; if you'll be teaching a procedure for solving linear equations, you might choose a flowchart or sequence organizer. The good news is that the most common organizers can be found online. For example, McREL International, one of the leading education research organizations in the world, has collected some of the most commonly used organizers at http://www.ascd.org/ASCD/pdf/books/dean2012_downloads.pdf.

Story maps are another type of graphic organizer (see Figure 7.7, p. 94) ideal for teaching students about narrative structure; they make the universal design elements that animate stories visible. They can be used to help younger students understand that nearly all stories contain common elements, and they can help students of all ages comprehend stories in all forms: in books, told by others, or viewed on movie, TV, or device screens. Story maps can also be used to build writing skills, guiding students as they plan and create their own fictional and narrative works.

Story maps can be modified in a number of ways, depending on your instructional goals and the age of your students. For example, one teacher we know focuses her students' attention on plot development with a story map that highlights the sequence and implications of key events. Her story map has eight boxes, each with a starter that students complete. The eight starters are *Someone . . . Somewhere . . . Wanted . . . But . . . So . . . Then . . . Therefore . . . Finally. . . .*

Concept maps, a third type of graphic organizer, teach students how to organize ideas and assimilate new learning in the same way that experts do: "around core concepts or 'big ideas' that guide their thinking about their domains" (National Research Council, 2000, p. 36). As a result, experts—and, by extension, students who learn to think like experts—can better store and call up relevant knowledge, enabling them to use that knowledge when they need it and transfer it to different contexts.

Concept maps are particularly effective in helping students make meaning when faced with complex or abstract material. Teaching students how

FIGURE 7.7

A Story Map

Name: _____   Date: _____

• Story Map •

Who are the MAIN CHARACTERS? Briefly describe them.

What is the SETTING? Describe *where* and *when* the story takes place.

What is the PROBLEM or conflict?

What is the sequence of EVENTS?
(First, next, then…)

How does the problem or conflict get resolved?
(RESOLUTION)

*Source: From Tools for Conquering the Common Core: Classroom-Ready Techniques for Targeting the ELA/
Literacy Standards (p. 73), by H. F. Silver and A. L. Boutz, 2015, Franklin Lakes, NJ: Silver Strong & Associates.*

to use concept maps means teaching them how to (1) start with a general (superordinate) concept, (2) arrange subordinate concepts hierarchically around the general concept, and (3) clarify the relationships between and among the concepts with linking lines and, more important, words that explain each relationship. Figure 7.8 presents an example of a concept map that a student created while learning about metric measurement. Notice how the map has the superordinate concept *matter* at the top, with relationships to and among the subordinate concepts shown visually with lines and explained briefly in words.

Concept maps can be used in several ways. They can be teacher-developed and used as advance organizers, or students can create their own maps to help them make meaning, represent their ideas, and synthesize

FIGURE 7.8

A Concept Map for Metric Measurement

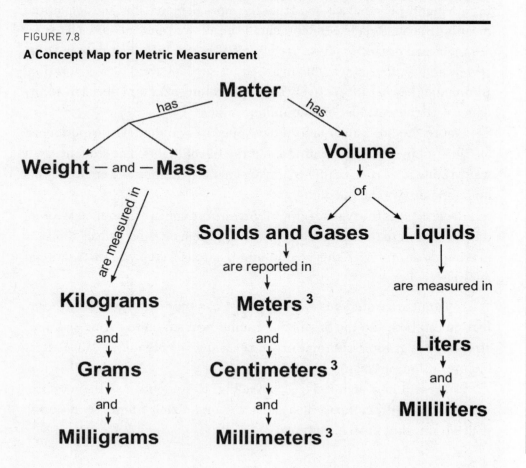

their learning. Student-created concept maps also serve as effective assessments by revealing the accuracy, completeness, and conceptual coherence of students' learning.

In essence, a concept map is a map of thinking. There are a variety of other predesigned thinking maps available to teachers. For example, visual learning expert David Hyerle (Hyerle & Yeager, 2017) has created a set of thinking maps representing different thinking processes that students can use to construct meaning and depict important ideas.

Student-generated visual organizers are the final type of graphic organizer we discuss here. Although established graphic organizers and thinking maps represent some of the most common forms that information and thinking can take, it is important to remember that meaning making is a highly personal act—and that the more personal it is, the deeper the meaning that gets made. Students should be allowed and encouraged to create their own organizers for a variety of purposes, including note making, review and synthesis, symbolizing abstract concepts, and idea generation. By doing so, learners are actively making meaning of new material in accordance with the workings of their unique minds.

Figure 7.9 shows an organizer developed by a student who experienced an "aha" moment while learning about the Bill of Rights. The student saw a way to build a "Garden of Rights," laying out both literally and creatively his understanding of the Bill of Rights.

Regardless of the types of graphic organizers you use in your classroom, it is important to teach students how to use them on their own as tools for making meaning. With this goal in mind, here is a stepwise instructional approach:

1. Familiarize students with the most common structures that information can take and the organizing frames best suited to various content structures (e.g., topic-subtopic organizer, sequence organizer, cause-effect organizer, concept map).

2. Present new material (e.g., a reading) to students. Ask them to preview the content, compare it against the organizing frames, and decide which frame best fits the content.

FIGURE 7.9

A Student-Generated Visual Organizer: The Garden of Rights

Source: From *So Each May Learn: Integrating Learning Styles and Multiple Intelligences* (p. 36), by H. F. Silver, R. W. Strong, and M. J. Perini, 2000, Alexandria, VA: ASCD. © 2000 Silver Strong & Associates. Used with permission.

3. Ask students to share and explain their choices. Remind them to refer to specific content to justify their choices (e.g., "I think a comparison frame is the best choice because the text explains how alligators and crocodiles are similar and different.").

4. Work with students to use (or create) the appropriate graphic organizer to collect the important information. Encourage them to continually ask themselves which information belongs where in the organizer—and to consider whether the organizer needs to be modified in any way to accommodate new information.

5. Challenge students to review their completed organizers by asking themselves, *Have I captured all the essential information? Do I have a big-picture understanding of the content? If not, what is still shaky or unclear in my mind?*

6. Use this process regularly so that students become increasingly adept at identifying how information is structured and using organizers to construct meaning.

Summing Up

The old saying about a picture being worth a thousand words may not be literally true, but the idea behind it definitely is—namely, that our brains can pack a lot of meaning into visual information, especially when we create it ourselves. But visualizing is more than creating mental images. It is also a way to organize and represent information so that the relationships within that information are clear. By using the tools in this chapter to help students build both these visualizing capacities, teachers can capitalize on the unique human ability to make complex information "seeable" and, therefore, easier to understand.

8

Perspective Taking and Empathizing

The *What* and *Why* of Perspective Taking and Empathizing

People familiar with the Charles Dickens classic *A Christmas Carol* will remember the main character, Ebenezer Scrooge, as a miserly misanthrope whose entire outlook on life is transformed overnight by his encounter with three ghosts. Dickens's ghosts help Scrooge gain a broader view of the world and his place in it, and they ignite his decision to become a better man. They accomplish all this by capitalizing on two uniquely human capacities: perspective and empathy.

The ghosts use *perspective* to change Scrooge's mind. By showing him episodes from his own past, revealing what life is like for most Londoners in the present, and forecasting what the future likely holds, the ghosts force Scrooge out of his selfish mindset. Concurrently, the ghosts rely on the power of *empathy* to bring about a change of heart. For Scrooge, reexperiencing the moment he lost his only love, witnessing the warmth of a humble family dinner, and enduring the unspeakable sadness of a child's death all conspire to help him "feel" again. The ghosts show Scrooge these things because they know full well—or, more accurately, Dickens knew full well—that to be human is to be able to empathize with fellow human beings.

Both perspective and empathy involve the human capacity to step out of our own egocentric frame and explore different points of view, but they are not the same. Let's explore each in turn, starting with perspective.

The ability to consider various perspectives is an analytical, evaluative capacity that undergirds critical thinking. Thinkers who value perspective recognize that their initial response may be influenced by limited information or unconscious biases and therefore do not rush to judgment. Instead, they deliberately seek out and consider different points of view before arriving at a conclusion. Wiggins and McTighe (2005) characterize this capacity through associated questions:

> Perspective involves the discipline of asking, *How does it look from another point of view? How, for example, would my critics see things? From whose point of view? From which vantage point? What is assumed that needs to be made explicit and considered? What is justified or warranted? Is there adequate evidence? Is it reasonable? What are the strengths and weaknesses of the idea? Is it plausible? What are its limits? So what?* (p. 96)

Perspective requires us to be open-minded and carefully consider views that may be different from ours. When students have perspective, they are able to assume a critical distance from the habitual beliefs and knee-jerk reactions that characterize less careful and circumspect thinkers. We can see the importance of perspective in nearly all contemporary academic standards. For example, various sets of science standards, including the National Science Education Standards (National Research Council, 1996) and the Next Generation Science Standards (National Research Council, 2013), call for learners to be able to view science from technological and engineering perspectives as well as to consider societal and ethical implications of scientific advances.

Whereas perspective is critical and analytical and involves viewing things dispassionately from a distance, empathy is more personal, emotional, and intimate. Empathetic understanding means being able to walk in someone else's shoes; thus, when we empathize, we are deeply aware of and sensitive to others' feelings, thoughts, and experiences. But empathy is not just about raw feeling. At its core, empathy requires respect for the "other," especially for people whose lives and worldviews differ from our own. This aspect of empathy is incorporated in the recommendations of the Bradley Commission on History in Schools (1988), a blue-ribbon panel assembled to improve the teaching of history. The commission's report declares that a primary aim of history is to help students escape their ethnocentric and present-centered views in order to develop empathy for people living in different places and times. Similarly, the Collaborative for Academic, Social, and Emotional Learning (CASEL) has identified "the ability to take the perspective of and empathize with others, including those from diverse backgrounds and cultures" (2017, para. 4) as one of its five core competencies.

Both perspective and empathy give teachers dynamic ways to enhance instruction and deepen students' understanding of people and ideas. Both processes require learners to move beyond basic knowledge and skills to actively construct deeper meaning. To grow in perspective is to cultivate critical thinking ability. To exhibit empathy is to show social-emotional maturity and make fundamental human connections. These ways of thinking can be fruitfully applied to many areas of the school curriculum. Perhaps most important, they are valuable meaning-making skills that students will need to use throughout their lives.

The *How* of Perspective Taking and Empathizing

Teachers can help students develop perspective by providing them with explicit opportunities to consider various points of view, diverse ideas, and alternative interpretations and conclusions. For example, you might ask students to consider the perspectives of different characters in a work of literature—especially characters whose points of view are not represented in the narrative. Consider using perspective-shifting retellings of well-known stories, such as John Scieszka's *The True Story of the 3 Little Pigs! (by A. Wolf),* to help students see the story another way. In health class, you might ask students to consider different perspectives on what "healthy eating" means. And one of our favorite essential questions in history—*Whose "story" is this?*—signals to students that history involves interpretation and that different people can view the same event very differently. In other words, to truly understand the past, students must deliberately consider differing perspectives, including *his*-story, *her*-story, and *their*-story.

When it comes to developing empathy in the classroom, we come almost immediately to a question: how can anyone *really* understand the experience of another without living through it? For example, can men ever empathize with the joys and agonies of childbirth? Can a person born into relative affluence ever truly understand the challenges of poverty? Arguably, deep empathy develops through shared experience. And in fact, some students may have immersive experiences (e.g., field trips, community service projects, peer counseling, volunteer programs, readers' theater, and some types of project-based learning) that offer close-up interactions with people who live very different lives from their own. Although such direct experiences do help students develop empathetic responses, they are not always available or practical to pursue. The good news is that teachers can also use indirect methods, including descriptive books or movies, role-playing, simulations, and dramatic enactments as a means of opening the door to empathy.

Figure 8.1 lists examples of how teachers of all grade levels and content areas can incorporate both perspective and empathy into their classrooms.

In addition to making these general recommendations, we present five practical tools and strategies to help students make meaning through perspective and empathy:

1. **Questioning Prompts** are simple cues for developing questions that engage learners in considering diverse perspectives and empathizing.

2. **Put the "You" in the Content** enhances students' development of perspective and empathy by having them look at content through the lens of their own experiences and values.

3. **Perspective Chart** encourages students to view the content they are studying through the perspectives of various stakeholders.

4. **Meeting of the Minds** and **Mock Trial** invite students to assume the roles of historic figures and literary characters to discuss and debate their ideas or defend their actions.

5. **A Day in the Life** helps students develop new insights by challenging them to "become" the people, ideas, and things they are learning about—and to use creative and personal forms of writing to describe the experience.

FIGURE 8.1

Using Perspective and Empathy Across the Curriculum

Business	• Consider product development and marketing from the perspectives of a manufacturer, a small-business owner, an investor, and a customer. • Consider how you would feel if you were cheated as a result of unscrupulous business practices. What might you do to address the situation?

Literature	• Consider the story from the viewpoint of a minor character. How might this character describe the situation?
	 • How might the story or the characters change if
	  – The story took place in a different setting or time period?
	  – *You* were the author?

Writing	• Write a persuasive essay for two very different audiences. How did changing the audience influence your argument, tone, word choice, or use of examples? • Write a modern-day version of a classic fairy tale or folktale.
Health	• Develop a personal fitness program for a middle-aged client who is a sedentary office worker with arthritic knees. Your program should include aerobic, anaerobic, and flexibility exercises. • Imagine and describe how your life would be different if you had a condition that required dietary restrictions (e.g., diabetes or lactose intolerance).
Mathematics	• Show the same data using different graphical scales (e.g., a truncated scale versus an expanded scale). What impressions do the various graphs convey? • Imagine a world with no fractions. How would everyday life be harder?
Science and Technology	• Examine the ethics of scientific and technological advances (e.g., cloning) from different perspectives (e.g., medical, theoretical, philosophical). • How does Aristotelian logic differ from Newtonian physics in its explanation of physical phenomena? • Imagine that you are an endangered species. Describe your experiences, thoughts, and feelings.
Social Studies	• Identify two or more significantly differing interpretations of a historical or current event. What are the different perspectives that influence these interpretations? • We just watched the movie *Amistad.* Imagine being a slave transported across the ocean on that ship. What would it be like to experience such atrocities? What would you be thinking and feeling?
Visual and Performing Arts	• Photograph the same event from different perspectives in ways that can significantly alter how people view the event. Describe how point of view influences the meanings people make. • What do you imagine [artist/singer/songwriter] was feeling when he or she composed this [artwork/song]?

Questioning Prompts

A natural way to encourage students to consider various perspectives and develop empathy for others is to use prompting questions. Questions and question stems such as the following can be used in conjunction with targeted standards and classroom activities to help students dig deeper into content, think critically about claims, and evoke empathy:

- What are different points of view about _____?
- How might this look from _____'s perspective?
- What are other possible reactions to _____?
- Whose "story" is this?
- What is the position of the other side?
- How would [another person, a different political party, a person from a different culture or time period, an alternative scientific theory] explain this?
- If you were to argue the other side of the case, what points would you make?
- Consider how you would feel if you were _____.
- What would it be like to walk in _____'s shoes?
- What advice would you give to _____?
- How might _____ feel about _____?
- What was the [artist, author, musician, film director] trying to make us feel/see?

Put the "You" in the Content

Allowing students to explore content through the lens of their own experiences and values not only engages students but also helps them recognize their commonalities, thereby creating the conditions for greater perspective and empathy. Indeed, while both perspective and empathy require students to step outside themselves, it is also true that both capacities can be enhanced through deeper understanding of the self.

Put the "You" in the Content is a reminder to make learning personal for students. It consists of a set of simple techniques that can be used to invite students' experiences, stories, and reactions into the classroom and use those personal elements as a springboard for developing perspective, empathy, and deeper understanding.

Personal Storytelling. Perhaps the simplest of these techniques, Personal Storytelling encourages students to tell the story of themselves. Can they describe an incident that helped make them who they are today? Is there a mentor, role model, or guiding voice that has shaped their thinking in a particular way? How has their cultural background, their family, a significant trial in their life, or a combination of these elements given direction or meaning to their lives? All these questions, and many others, can serve as the basis for rich personal stories. And don't forget to have students share their stories. After all, it is by sharing our strengths, fears, and challenges that we begin to understand our commonality.

You Are There. This technique, which uses the self (along with perspective and empathy) to enhance learning, was inspired by the 1950s TV show of the same name. Hosted by the legendary newscaster Walter Cronkite, the show featured reenactments of famous historic events, with a reporter asking questions to learn more about the event and explore the thoughts and feelings of those involved. You can easily adopt this premise in your classroom to bring history and literature to life. Try having students imagine that they "are there" by assuming the roles of historic or literary characters to be interviewed or conducting interviews with the characters (or the students who are playing them) in the event. For example, imagine interviewing King Tutankhamen or a slave in colonial America. What questions would you ask? What might each say in response?

Think of a Time. Adapted from the work of Faye Brownlie, Susan Close, and Linda Wingren (1990), Think of a Time is designed to help students see content from different points of view. Specifically, students are asked to examine an issue from three points of view: as a participant, as an observer, and as a supporter.

To make this process come to life in the classroom, think of each point of view as a round. For example, suppose you want students to develop a deeper understanding of prejudice and how it affects people. You would group students into teams of three; number the students in each group as One, Two, and Three; and then proceed through three rounds.

First Round: Students think of a time when they were *participants* (e.g., when they personally confronted prejudice). Students record their experiences in writing, compare their experiences with those of their team members, and try to determine some common attributes of prejudice based on their collective experiences. After exploring the various points of view of the three team members, all Number One students form another team, where they take turns sharing their original teams' ideas. Members of the new group share and compare their original groups' conclusions.

Second Round: The process is repeated from the second point of view. Students think of a time when they were *observers* (e.g., when they observed someone experiencing prejudice). Again, student teams record and discuss their experiences. Then all Number Two students move to a new group and compare ideas in the same manner as the first round.

Third Round: Finally, students consider the topic from the *supporter* perspective (e.g., what it was like when they supported someone who was experiencing prejudice). Again, students record and discuss their experiences. Then the Number Three students move to a new group and develop a final set of attributes or elements of prejudice based on their learning in all three rounds.

The process is typically concluded with a whole-class discussion in which students reflect on their learning and the process.

Perspective Chart

Many young people (and some older ones) view the world predominantly through the lens of their own experiences and culture. The Perspective Chart (McTighe, 1996b) has proven to be a useful organizer that reminds learners to deliberately consider ways in which others might view a given situation or issue. This tool can be used to help students expand their perspective and come to a deeper understanding of an idea or appreciate the complexities of an issue. Figure 8.2 offers an example of a Perspective

FIGURE 8.2

Perspective Chart: Westward Expansion

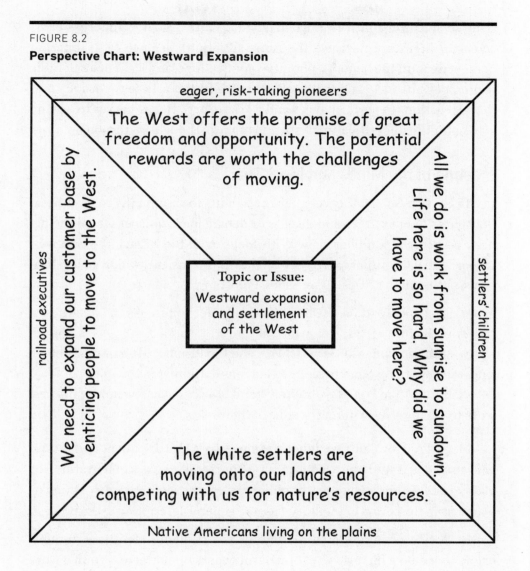

eager, risk-taking pioneers

The West offers the promise of great freedom and opportunity. The potential rewards are worth the challenges of moving.

railroad executives

We need to expand our customer base by enticing people to move to the West.

Topic or Issue:

Westward expansion and settlement of the West

settlers' children

All we do is work from sunrise to sundown. Life here is so hard. Why did we have to move here?

The white settlers are moving onto our lands and competing with us for nature's resources.

Native Americans living on the plains

Chart used in a social studies unit to help learners consider the impact of the settlement of the American West from different vantage points.

Perspective Chart is a versatile tool that can be applied across the content areas, including history (e.g., differing interpretations of past events); current events (e.g., how different constituent groups view a controversial issue such as gun control); English language arts (e.g., how different characters in literature perceive the same situation); science (e.g., different perspectives on the benefits, potential applications, and risks of a scientific technology such as artificial intelligence); and the arts (e.g., various aesthetic reactions to performances and works of art). Its use serves to expand viewpoints, foster critical analysis, and nurture thoughtful responses.

Meeting of the Minds and Mock Trial

These two related tools challenge students to assume the roles of notable figures or characters and discuss or debate ideas or issues from the figures' respective points of view. With Meeting of the Minds, the goal is to explore the various perspectives to achieve consensus, develop generalizations, or highlight critical differences. For example:

• Frog and Toad meet Charlotte the spider to discuss the qualities of true friendship.

• Mahatma Gandhi, Jesus Christ, and the Prophet Muhammad debate the best ways to respond to violent religious extremism.

• Edgar Allan Poe, Ray Bradbury, and Shirley Jackson explore the best ways to make readers sit on the edge of their seats.

Mock Trial, by contrast, tends to spur debate and argument and is typically used when studying a historic period or reading a work of literature as a class. Students investigate real or potential "crimes" committed by key characters from the period or the story. Here's a general description of the process:

1. The teacher proposes a crime or the students identify a possible crime based on a historic situation or on events or characters from a work of literature. For example, students in an English class might put Hamlet on trial for the murder of Polonius, while students in a history class might put a famous leader on trial for abuse of power. Charges are then brought against the defendant.

2. Students are divided into groups with specific roles (e.g., prosecutors and defense attorneys), and allowed time to prepare their case for or against the defendant. They must assemble evidence based on authoritative

sources (e.g., information grounded in the literary text or based on historic information) and develop the argument for their side of the case.

3. The trial is conducted following general courtroom procedures, which need to be reviewed in advance. You may choose to play the role of a judge, invite a guest judge (e.g., a librarian or vice principal), or have a student serve as judge. To create a more authentic "courtroom," rearrange the room to include a judge's bench, a witness stand, an area for the prosecution and defense teams, and a jury box. You can even provide a gavel for the judge to use to maintain order in the court.

Some tips for conducting effective classroom trials include the following:

• For students unfamiliar with how a mock trial works, videos can illustrate the process. YouTube offers many useful clips, including one showing the elements and procedures of a mock trial (Texas Youth & Government Training Videos, 2014; available at www.youtube.com/watch?v =qtQDOQM4dM8) and, for younger students, the story of Goldilocks and the Three Bears played out as a mock trial (SETV, 2011; available at www. youtube.com/watch?v=qw7Z4dLkPko).

• To make sure all students are involved, you might run two trials to allow every student to have a speaking role in one trial and to serve as a juror for the other trial.

• For large classes, you might select a few students to serve as "process observers" to take notes during the trial and offer feedback on how other students played their roles.

A Day in the Life

A Day in the Life asks students to imagine life as a famous figure or character, or even as a concept or an object they're learning about. In addition to helping students develop new insights into the content, this tool stimulates creative thinking and writing and cultivates empathetic responses to the content under investigation.

When using the tool to help students "become" other people, it is a good idea to ask students to tell their day-in-the-life story through personal writing (e.g., diary entries or a letter to a friend) that captures the viewpoint of their adopted figure. For younger students, the product might take the form of an illustration or a picture book. Here are two examples:

• You have watched the documentary *Life in the Trenches,* about trench warfare during World War I, and read the poem "In Flanders Fields." Choose one of the following roles: a frightened new arrival, an officer trying to bolster troop morale, or a nurse in a field hospital. Write a letter back home describing your experiences.

• We have just completed our unit on biography and learned that one of the defining attributes of a good biography is showing how people overcome challenges. Pick the biographical story that you liked best from this unit. Try to identify the figure's greatest challenge. Then be that person, writing two or three diary entries that give us insight into what you were thinking and what you decided to do to overcome your challenge.

When used with objects or concepts instead of characters, A Day in the Life challenges students to stretch their imaginations even further—to get beyond their familiar world and to look at content from a new and unusual perspective. To use the tool in this way, identify an object or a concept related to the topic you are teaching as the basis for students' thinking and writing. Depending on your goals, student responses can be short and sweet, or they may serve as the basis for extended thinking and writing. In all cases, students should use first-person ("I") narration. Here are some examples:

• Imagine you are a white blood cell. You and your friends have received an emergency 911 call to rush to battle a new virus that has invaded the body you inhabit. Describe your process of finding and destroying the enemy virus.

• Imagine you are the application of an immigrant seeking asylum in a Western democracy. You find yourself caught in a tug of war between pro-immigration and anti-immigration factions. Make sure your story reveals the arguments on both sides as well as your personal feelings about your future being tied up in the debate.

• You are a chrysalis that just can't wait to become a butterfly. Explain what life is like for you as you await your transformation. Make sure you tell us what excites you most about becoming a butterfly.

Once students get the hang of this technique, you can invite them to create their own day-in-the-life narratives related to content of their choice within a lesson or unit. We think you'll be pleasantly surprised with some of the unique connections that kids can make!

Summing Up

Perspective taking and empathizing are two distinct but related ways of examining the world around us. But they are also ideal meaning-making skills, because when we use them to drive learning in the classroom, we are encouraging students to use both their minds and their hearts to build their understanding. Using the tools in this chapter, teachers can help students connect to the human component in what they are learning, leading students to a deeper understanding of themselves, others, and the content under investigation.

9

Putting It All Together

So far in this book, we've discussed the importance of framing classroom content around big ideas and presented a diverse collection of thinking skills and associated tools that you can use to help students make meaning of that content. In this concluding chapter, we help you put it all together by describing (1) a tried-and-true protocol for teaching students how to apply thinking skills and tools on their own, (2) an instructional design framework that can help you decide which skills and tools to apply within individual lessons and units, and (3) a mapping process for deliberately integrating a range of skills and tools into your curriculum over the course of an entire year.

Developing Students' Capacity to Apply Skills and Tools Independently

Teachers can use the instructional tools we've presented to help learners make meaning of what they're learning and develop understandings that last. However, the tools aren't just for teachers. In fact, the ultimate goal is transfer—that is, empowering students to become proficient enough users of the tools that they'll be able to apply these tools (and the embedded thinking skills) independently in future learning situations. Thus, it's just as important to help students incorporate the tools into *their* repertoires as it is for you to build them into yours. We have found that the best way to do this is to teach the tools directly. Figure 9.1 presents an explicit five-step process for teaching individual tools to students.

FIGURE 9.1

Teaching a Tool in Five Steps

Basic Steps	How to Execute the Steps
1. Prepare students for new learning.	• Before teaching, review the tool carefully. Make sure you understand it. • Explain the purpose of the tool to students.
2. Present and model the basic steps.	• Present the tool one step at a time. • Explain and model the individual steps. Think aloud as you model.
3. Deepen and reinforce student understanding.	• Have students practice using the tool with guidance from you. • Use ongoing (formative) assessment to determine whether students are ready to use the tool independently. • Provide additional instruction as needed.
4. Challenge students to apply the tool.	• Assign a simple task that requires students to use the tool. • Assess students' skill level and provide coaching as needed. • Look for further opportunities to have students use the tool in more sophisticated ways. • Encourage students to use the tool on their own—not just when you tell them to (e.g., "Follow these steps *whenever* you're asked to conduct a comparison.").
5. Help students reflect on and celebrate their use of the tool.	• Pose questions like these to help students reflect on their use of the tool: *What came easily? What was challenging? How did using the tool enhance your thinking and understanding? What other kinds of tasks might the tool help you tackle? How might you improve your use of the tool the next time around?* • Celebrate students' successful use of the tool.

Building an Instructional Unit

Now let's turn our attention to instructional design. Because one of the best ways to learn is by example, we'll show you how a middle school teacher pulled together strategies and tools from this book to create a thoughtful and engaging unit on the rainforest. This unit is focused around big ideas as advised in Chapter 1, incorporates the thinking skills and tools discussed in Chapters 2–8, and reflects the principles of effective instructional design. The scenario that follows will let you get inside this teacher's head so you can understand the decision-making processes and motivations that led her to design the unit the way she did. It will also introduce you to a lesson/unit design framework (Silver Strong & Associates, 2013) that you can use to map out your own lessons and units in a way that promotes deep and lasting learning and engagement. Built on research into how learners develop deep understanding (Goodwin, Gibson, Lewis, & Rouleau, 2018), this framework also incorporates design elements from some of the most highly regarded instructional models (Dean et al., 2012; Hunter, 1984; Marzano, 2007; Wiggins & McTighe, 2005). The framework encourages teachers to think about instructional design as a series of five phases, or "episodes," each with its own purpose—and to map out the instructional tools and activities that they'll use during each episode. Figure 9.2 (p. 117) shows how the teacher used this framework to organize her unit around big ideas and engage her students in making meaning of the relevant content.

This is not the first time I have taught a unit on the rainforest. But after attending one of Jay and Harvey's workshops, I was motivated to change my approach, since I realized that I had been designing my unit around activities rather than around the big ideas I wanted my students to understand. So this time, I "began with the end in mind" by asking myself, "What are the big ideas I want my students to walk away with?" A favorite quotation from Margaret Mead helped guide my thinking: ". . . recognize and respect Earth's beautiful systems of balance, between the presence of animals on land, the fish in the sea, birds in the air, mankind, water, air, and land. Most importantly there must always be awareness of the actions by people that can disturb this precious balance" [Nath, 2009, p. 265].

Mead's words brought to mind one of the crosscutting concepts in our science standards: *systems*. I realized that I wanted my students to understand that the rainforest is an example of a harmonious and interdependent system, in which any change in one part of the system can affect the system as a whole. Specifically, I wanted them to appreciate that the living things in an ecosystem are interdependent and that an ecosystem needs to be balanced in order to survive and thrive. Another big idea I wanted my students to understand is that there's interdependence and balance not just *within* the rainforest but *between* the rainforest and the rest of the world—in other words, that the health and existence of the rainforest impacts the health and existence of those outside the rainforest (including my students!). By encouraging students to begin thinking about the importance of the rainforest to them and to the rest of the world and about actions that they and others could take to preserve the balance of nature that Mead was referring to, I felt that I could make the unit more personally relevant and engaging.

Thinking through the big ideas that I wanted my students to understand helped me see that my unit really represented a study in the balance and harmony of nature, so I titled my unit accordingly using **A Study In . . .** [p. 8]. I believe that presenting my unit as "The Rainforest: A Study in Balance and Harmony" will keep my students and me focused on the core concepts. To further ensure that teaching and learning stay focused on big ideas, I used the **Essential Questions** approach [p. 10] to develop three questions that would drive exploration of the core ideas and understandings I wanted students to develop:

1. How can small changes in a system have a dramatic impact on the entire system?
2. How do living things depend on one another for survival?
3. Why should I care about faraway people, places, and issues?

I worked hard to frame my rainforest content around broader, more universal concepts and questions so that my students will be able to transfer the understandings they develop in this unit to other contexts and content areas.

With Jay's voice in my head reminding me that thoughtful unit design requires getting clarity not just about what you want students to understand but also about how you'll determine whether they "got" those understandings, I started thinking about a culminating assessment task that would challenge students to apply (and let me assess) their understanding of the big ideas and questions that we were going to be exploring. I decided to have students select and research an issue that's threatening the world's rainforests (e.g., deforestation), explain what the problem is and how it will negatively impact the rainforest ecosystem or the world, and make a case for funding solutions to their selected issue. To make the task more engaging, interactive, and authentic, I decided to set it up as a simulated United Nations World Summit.

Once I was clear about my big ideas, essential questions, and culminating assessment, I used the five episodes from the Thoughtful Classroom Lesson/Unit Design Framework [Silver Strong & Associates, 2013] to map out my unit and identify the specific activities and tools that I'd use to help students make meaning of the relevant content. Once my unit plan was complete, I checked that the activities I had planned were aligned with the big ideas and essential questions I had identified in the beginning—in other words, that they were purposeful activities and not just activities we'd do for the sake of doing them.

I think the way I planned the unit this time around—focusing it around big ideas rather than activities and incorporating instructional tools that will engage students in actively processing the content—is going to make a big difference in student learning. I'm enthusiastic about the work I've done, and I'm excited to get teaching! I think my students will be excited to get learning, too.

Mapping a Full Year's Curriculum

Our final goal in this chapter is to encourage you to think beyond individual lessons or units, and consider an entire school year. Here's an analogy: think of your curriculum as a patchwork quilt. Individual patches or squares are like units, containing interwoven lessons. The individual lessons may be well crafted, and the units may be thoughtfully composed (like the rainforest unit we just examined) to infuse specific thinking skills and tools that engage learners in making meaning of the content. But do these individual

FIGURE 9.2

Using the Five-Episode Framework to Plan a Unit on the Rainforest

Instructional Episodes	The Rainforest: A Study in Balance and Harmony Instructional Sequence
1. Preparing students for new learning	Post and introduce core concept words (e.g., *harmony, interdependence, balance, adaptation*) using the **Concept Word Wall** tool (p. 9). Help students "experience" and begin to understand some of the words by having them build a rainforest mobile with their classmates that requires *balancing* the parts and working *harmoniously* and *interdependently* with their peers. Have students use the core concept words to describe what they did (e.g., "We had to work *harmoniously* to *balance* the pieces."). K-W-L: Have students record what they *Know* and *Want* to know about the rainforest. Present the unit as **A Study In** (p. 8) Balance and Harmony. Introduce the **Essential Questions** (p. 10).
2. Presenting new learning	Show a video about the rainforest and its importance to the world. Use prompts from **Reading Stances** (p. 61) to have students process and discuss the material. Have students read an article on the layers of the rainforest and how plants and animals are adapted to specific layers. Use **Reading for Meaning** (p. 65) to help them read more closely and explore the critical concepts. Have them create a **Graphic Organizer** (p. 91) to synthesize their understanding of the layers and organisms that live there. Develop and test their grasp of the adaptation concept with **Yes, But Why?** (p. 71): Yes, different things live in each layer. But why? Take students to the rainforest exhibit at the zoo. Spark interest and engagement before going with a **Prediction-Based Hook** (p. 71) that asks them to predict what they might learn at the zoo that they didn't learn from either the reading or the video (e.g., how a rainforest smells or how the humidity feels). Have them make **Window Notes** (p. 31) about what they see during their visit. Ask them to compare their predictions with what they actually learned.
3. Deepening and reinforcing learning	Have students synthesize and personalize their learning by researching and then pretending to be a particular plant or animal and describing **A Day in the Life** (p. 109) of that organism— where it lives, how it meets its needs, what it eats (or gets eaten by), and so on. Encourage the use of rich, sensory language by giving students examples of such writing to use as models. Have students use **Describe First, Compare Second** (p. 46) to compare their wants, needs, and interactions with those of their chosen animal or plant. The goal is to develop students' understanding of interdependence by helping them see that all living things depend on other creatures and resources to fulfill their basic needs. Use **What If?** (p. 71) questions to develop and test students' grasp of interdependence and adaptation—for example, *What if your plant or animal ceased to exist? What if the rainforest were damaged by deforestation—how would it impact your organism's survival?* Use **Visualizing Vocabulary** (p. 89) to challenge students to create a simple image or symbol that reflects their understanding of interdependence.
4. Applying and demonstrating learning	Assessment task: Create a model UN World Summit where students will describe an issue that's threatening the rainforest, explain how it negatively impacts the rainforest or world, propose a plan for addressing the issue, and make a case for why their plan is worth funding.
5. Reflecting on and celebrating learning	Have students complete the "what I *Learned*" portion of their K-W-L chart, reflect on whether they learned what they had *Wanted* to, and identify questions to pursue further. Present the Margaret Mead quotation that I used to focus my thinking about this unit. Reflect as a class on its meaning and how Mead's words resonate with us based on what we learned.

patches contribute to the overall mosaic and cohere into a coordinated quilt? To address this question, we recommend using a Mapping Matrix as a planning tool for organizing a full year's curriculum.

What Is a Mapping Matrix, and Why Use It?

The standards in most disciplines feature the confluence of content and process. For example, the Common Core State Standards for Mathematics include both grade-level standards that specify the mathematical content and Standards for Mathematical Practice, which identify the process skills. Similarly, the Next Generation Science Standards include science content (in the form of disciplinary core ideas and crosscutting concepts) along with science and engineering practices (process skills). Standards from other disciplines (e.g., the C3 Social Studies Standards and the National Core Arts Standards) are similarly constructed.

The structure of these standards is purposeful—to remind teachers that simply transmitting factual information about various content topics is insufficient. Instead, the standards intend for teachers to involve students in "doing" the subject by applying the key processes (practices) as they are learning the content. Accordingly, a matrix is a tool perfectly suited for mapping a curriculum for an entire school year because it allows key standards and content topics to be listed on the vertical axis and process skills (practices) to be listed on the horizontal axis. The "cells" of the matrix can then be used to plan for and display the confluence of content and process—exactly what the standards expect!

The Mapping Matrix we present here also features the confluence of content and process, but it's designed to do more than that. Specifically, it will help you incorporate the thinking skills and tools from this book as you map out your curriculum. The Mapping Matrix has three primary purposes:

1. *To help ensure that all your units throughout the year are framed around transferable big ideas and essential questions.* Without a focus on conceptually large ideas, it is too easy to simply map the curriculum around lists of topics and discrete facts and skills. Such an approach can lead to "coverage" teaching and result in superficial and fragmented learning.

2. *To remind you of the importance of actively engaging learners in making meaning of key ideas in the content.* By aligning designated content from your instructional units with specific thinking skills and associated tools, you increase the likelihood that students will actively engage and achieve deeper, more enduring learning.

3. *To help you systematically give students multiple opportunities to apply meaning-making skills and tools over the course of an entire school year.* A one-shot exposure to any skill or tool is unlikely to build competency. However, when students have repeated opportunities to apply the skills using a variety of tools, they develop increased proficiency in the independent use of both the skills and the tools.

How Can Teachers Use a Mapping Matrix?

To help you envision how to use our Mapping Matrix, take a look at the example for a full-year course on American History in Figure 9.3 (p. 120). The left-hand column (vertical axis) offers a place to map out the *content* by identifying the unit topics for the year. The top row (horizontal axis) is *process*-oriented and asks you to consider two process-related instructional design questions:

1. *How will I frame the content around big ideas?* (Use the two columns below this question to frame unit topics around conceptually big ideas using A Study In . . . and associated Essential Questions.)

2. *How will I ensure that students actively make meaning of content?* (Use the two columns below this question to specify the thinking skills and associated tools that you think will best help students achieve deep learning of the unit's content.)

Note that this matrix does not include the history standards addressed, because local, state, national, and international standards vary. However, a standards column can easily be added to the content axis of a mapping matrix.

This matrix clearly shows the alignment among topics, core concepts, and essential questions. It also helps curriculum planners see which skills and tools will be used to ensure that all relevant skills are being addressed

FIGURE 9.3

A Curriculum Mapping Matrix for an American History Course (1890 to Present)

PROCESS ▶ How will I frame the content around big ideas?			How will I ensure that students actively make meaning of content?	
CONTENT ▼				
Unit Topics	*A Study In . . .*	**Essential Questions**	**Skills***	**Tools**
Historical Inquiry and Historiography	Meaning making	• How do we know what really happened in the past? • Whose "story" is this? • What does it mean?	√ CON __ NMS __ COM √ RU √ PH __ VGR __ PTE	• Concept Attainment • Reading for Meaning • Inductive Learning • If-Then
Industrialization and Immigration	Upheaval	• Who were the "winners and losers" during the Industrial Age? • Why do people move? • What happens when cultures intermix?	√ CON __ NMS √ COM √ RU __ PH __ VGR √ PTE	• Scavenger Hunt • Adding Up the Facts • Compare and Conclude Matrix • A Day in the Life
American Imperialism and World War I	Expansion	• American imperialism: A force for liberation or oppression? • Was the "Great War" inevitable?	√ CON √ NMS __ COM __ RU __ PH __ VGR √ PTE	• Window Notes • Concept Definition Map • Perspective Chart
The Progressive Era	Reforms	• What is government's responsibility in achieving a just society?	√ CON __ NMS __ COM √ RU __ PH __ VGR √ PTE	• Concept Definition Map • Reading Stances • Perspective Chart • Community CIRCLE
The Great Depression	Greed	• Why did it happen? • Could it happen again?	__ CON √ NMS __ COM √ RU __ PH __ VGR √ PTE	• Reading Stances • 4-2-1 Summarize • You Are There
World War II	Decisions	• When (if ever) should we go to war? • Is war ever just?	√ CON __ NMS __ COM __ RU __ PH √ VGR √ PTE	• Adding Up the Facts • Mind's Eye • Put the "You" in the Content • Meeting of the Minds
The Cold War	Rivalries	• Are we still in a cold war?	√ CON __ NMS √ COM √ RU __ PH √ VGR __ PTE	• Power Previewing • Graphic Organizers • Connect-the-Concepts • Compare and Conclude Matrix
The Politics of Division	Clashing views	• How do the ideals of liberalism and conservativism come into conflict?	√ CON __ NMS √ COM √ RU __ PH __ VGR √ PTE	• Concept Definition Map • Reading Stances • Perspective Chart • Community CIRCLE

*Key to thinking skills: CON = Conceptualizing, NMS = Note Making and Summarizing, COM = Comparing, RU = Reading for Understanding, PH = Predicting and Hypothesizing, VGR = Visualizing and Graphic Representation, PTE = Perspective Taking and Empathizing throughout the course and that students get sufficient practice using the skills so that they're able to apply (transfer) them to future learning.

Conclusion: Now It's Your Turn

In this book, we have made the case for engaging learners in active meaning making to promote deep learning. To move from "making the case" to helping you "make it real in the classroom," we have presented a set of seven thinking skills, along with ready-to-use tools to make the meaning-making process come alive in classrooms; we have provided guidance on how to frame your curriculum around big ideas; and we have offered suggestions on how to integrate the skills and tools into your lessons, units, and year-long courses. So what is left to do? Only one thing, and it is your charge: to begin the essential work of helping students make meaning for themselves, so that they can succeed in school, thrive in their careers, and stand prepared for the complex challenges of the world that await them.

References

Beesley, A., & Apthorp, H. (Eds.). (2010). *Classroom instruction that works, second edition: Research report*. Denver, CO: Mid-continent Research for Education and Learning.

Boutz, A. L., Silver, H. F., Jackson, J. W., & Perini, M. J. (2012). *Tools for thoughtful assessment: Classroom-ready techniques for improving teaching and learning*. Franklin Lakes, NJ: Silver Strong & Associates/Thoughtful Education Press.

Boyle, J. (2013). Strategic note-taking for inclusive middle school science classrooms. *Remedial and Special Education, 34*(2), 78–90.

Bradley Commission on History in Schools. (1988). *Building a history curriculum: Guidelines for teaching history in schools*. Westlake, OH: National Council for History Education. Retrieved from https://www.nche.net/bradleyreport

Brownlie, F., Close, S., & Wingren, L. (1990). *Tomorrow's classrooms today: Strategies for creating active readers, writers, and thinkers*. Portsmouth, NH: Heinemann.

Brownlie, F., & Silver, H. F. (1995). *Mind's eye*. Paper presented at the seminar Responding Thoughtfully to the Challenge of Diversity, Delta, Canada.

Bruner, J. (1973). *Beyond the information given: Studies in the psychology of knowing*. Oxford: W. W. Norton.

Collaborative for Academic, Social, and Emotional Learning (CASEL). (2017). Core SEL competencies. Retrieved from https://casel.org/core-competencies

Dean, C. B., Hubbell, E. R., Pitler, H., & Stone, B. (2012). *Classroom instruction that works: Research-based strategies for increasing student achievement* (2nd ed.). Alexandria, VA: ASCD.

Erickson, H. L. (2007). *Concept-based curriculum and instruction for the thinking classroom*. Thousand Oaks, CA: Corwin.

Erickson, H. L. (2008). *Stirring the head, heart, and soul: Redefining curriculum, instruction, and concept-based learning* (3rd ed.). Thousand Oaks, CA: Corwin.

Erickson, H. L., Lanning, L. A., & French, R. (2017). *Concept-based curriculum and instruction for the thinking classroom* (2nd ed.). Thousand Oaks, CA: Corwin.

Flammer, L., Beard, J., Nelson, C. E., & Nickels, M. (n.d.). Science preparation for elementary school students. Retrieved from http://www.indiana.edu/~ensiweb/Sci.Prep.Elem.School.pdf

Goodwin, B., Gibson, T., Lewis, D., & Rouleau, K. (2018). *Unstuck: How curiosity, peer coaching, and teaming can change your school*. Alexandria, VA: ASCD.

Guido, B., & Colwell, C. G. (1987). A rationale for direct instruction to teach summary writing following expository text reading. *Reading Research and Instruction, 26,* 89–98.

Hattie, J., & Donoghue, G. (2016). Learning strategies: A synthesis and conceptual model. *npj Science of Learning, 1,* 16013. Retrieved from https://www.nature.com/articles/npjscilearn201613.pdf

Hunter, M. (1984). Knowing, teaching, and supervising. In P. Hosford (Ed.), *Using what we know about teaching* (pp. 169–192). Alexandria, VA: ASCD.

Hyerle, D., & Yeager, C. (2017). *Thinking maps: A language for learning* (2nd ed.). Cary, NC: Thinking Maps.

Langer, J. A. (1994). A response-based approach to reading literature. *Language Arts, 71*(3), 203–211.

Marzano, R. J. (2007). *The art and science of teaching: A comprehensive framework for effective instruction.* Alexandria, VA: ASCD.

Marzano, R. J. (2009). The art and science of teaching: Six steps to better vocabulary instruction. *Educational Leadership, 67*(1), 83–84.

Marzano, R. J., Pickering, D., & Pollock, J. (2001). *Classroom instruction that works: Research-based strategies for increasing student achievement.* Alexandria, VA: ASCD.

McTighe, J. (1996a). *Developing students' thinking skills* [Workshop handout]. Columbia, MD: McTighe & Associates.

McTighe, J. (1996b). Perspective chart. In *Improving the quality of student thinking* [Workshop materials]. Columbia, MD: McTighe & Associates.

McTighe, J. (2016). *Essential questions quick reference guide.* Alexandria, VA: ASCD.

McTighe, J., & Wiggins, G. (2013). *Essential questions: Opening doors to student understanding.* Alexandria, VA: ASCD.

McTighe, J., & Willis, J. (2019). *Upgrade your teaching: Understanding by Design meets neuroscience.* Alexandria, VA: ASCD.

Medina, J. (2008). *Brain rules.* Seattle, WA: Pear Press.

Nath, B. (Ed.). (2009). *Encyclopedia of life support systems: Environmental education and awareness.* Oxford: Eolss.

National Research Council. (1996). *National science education standards.* Washington, DC: National Academies Press.

National Research Council. (2000). *How people learn: Brain, mind, experience, and school* (Expanded ed.). Washington, DC: National Academies Press.

National Research Council. (2013). *Next generation science standards: For states, by states.* Washington, DC: National Academies Press.

Paivio, A. (1990). *Mental representations: A dual coding approach.* New York: Oxford University Press.

Pressley, M. (1979). *The mind's eye.* Escondido, CA: Escondido Union School District.

Pressley, M. (2006). *Reading instruction that works: The case for balanced teaching* (3rd ed.). New York: Guilford Press.

Rahmani, M., & Sadeghi, K. (2011). Effects of note-taking training on reading comprehension and recall. *The Reading Matrix, 11*(2). Retrieved from http://www.readingmatrix.com/articles/april_2011/rahmani_sadeghi.pdf

Robinson, F. P. (1946). *Effective study.* New York: Harper & Row.

Schmoker, M. (2018). *Focus: Elevating the essentials to radically improve student learning* (2nd ed.). Alexandria, VA: ASCD.

Schwartz, R. M., & Raphael, T. E. (1985). Concept of definition: A key to improving students' vocabulary. *The Reading Teacher, 39*(2), 198–205.

SETV (Saginaw County, Michigan, Public Schools). (2011, October 31). *"State v. Golden Locks" mock trial* [Video]. Retrieved from https://www.youtube.com/watch?v=qw7Z4dLkPko

Silver, H. F. (2010). *Compare & contrast: Teaching comparative thinking to strengthen student learning.* Alexandria, VA: ASCD.

Silver, H. F., Abla, C., Boutz, A. L., & Perini, M. J. (2018). *Tools for classroom instruction that works: Ready-to-use techniques for increasing student achievement.* Franklin Lakes, NJ: Silver Strong & Associates/Thoughtful Education Press and McREL International.

Silver, H. F., & Boutz, A. L. (2015). *Tools for conquering the Common Core: Classroom-ready techniques for targeting the ELA/literacy standards.* Franklin Lakes, NJ: Silver Strong & Associates/Thoughtful Education Press.

Silver, H. F., Brunsting, J. R., Walsh, T., & Thomas, E. J. (2012). *Math tools, grades 3–12: 60+ ways to build mathematical practices, differentiate instruction, and increase student engagement* (2nd ed.). Thousand Oaks, CA: Corwin.

Silver, H. F., Dewing, R. T., & Perini, M. J. (2012). *The core six: Essential strategies for achieving excellence with the Common Core.* Alexandria, VA: ASCD.

Silver, H. F., Morris, S. C., & Klein, V. (2010). *Reading for meaning: How to build students' comprehension, reasoning, and problem-solving skills.* Alexandria, VA: ASCD.

Silver, H. F., & Perini, M. J. (2010). *Classroom curriculum design: How strategic units improve instruction and engage students in meaningful learning.* Franklin Lakes, NJ: Thoughtful Education Press.

Silver, H. F., Perini, M. J., & Boutz, A. L. (2016). *Tools for a successful school year (starting on day one): Classroom-ready techniques for building the four cornerstones of an effective classroom.* Franklin Lakes, NJ: Silver Strong & Associates/Thoughtful Education Press.

Silver, H. F., Perini, M. J., & Gilbert, J. M. (2008). *The ten attributes of successful learners: Mastering the tools of learning.* Ho-Ho-Kus, NJ: Thoughtful Education Press.

Silver Strong & Associates. (2013). *The thoughtful classroom teacher effectiveness framework* (Resource guide). Ho-Ho-Kus, NJ: Author.

Silver Strong & Associates. (2018). *Power previewing* (poster). Franklin Lakes, NJ: Author.

Silver, H. F., Strong, R. W., & Perini, M. J. (2000). *So each may learn: Integrating learning styles and multiple intelligences.* Alexandria, VA: ASCD.

Silver, H. F., Strong, R. W., & Perini, M. J. (2007). *The strategic teacher: Selecting the right research-based strategy for every lesson.* Alexandria, VA: ASCD.

Stern, J., Ferraro, K., & Mohnkern, J. (2017). *Tools for teaching conceptual understanding: Designing lessons and assessments for deep learning.* Thousand Oaks, CA: Corwin.

Stone, B. (2016, September 1). Four tips for using nonlinguistic representations [Blog post]. Retrieved from https://www.mcrel.org/four-tips-for-using-nonlinguistic-representations

Taba, H., Durkin, M. C., Fraenkel, J. R., & McNaughton, A. H. (1971). *A teacher's handbook to elementary social studies: An inductive approach* (2nd ed.). Reading, MA: Addison-Wesley.

Texas Youth & Government Training Videos. (2014, October 9). *Example mock trial flow* [Video]. Retrieved from https://www.youtube.com/watch?v=qtDOQM4dM8

Thoughtful Education Press. (2007). *From note taking to notemaking: How making notes and summarizing strengthen student learning.* Franklin Lakes, NJ: Author.

Thoughtful Education Press. (2008). *Word works: Cracking vocabulary's CODE* (2nd ed.). Franklin Lakes, NJ: Author.

Wiggins, G. (1989). The futility of trying to teach everything of importance. *Educational Leadership, 47*(3), 45–49.

Wiggins, G., & McTighe, J. (2005). *Understanding by Design* (Expanded 2nd ed.). Alexandria, VA: ASCD.

Wiggins, G., & McTighe, J. (2011). *The Understanding by Design guide to creating high-quality units.* Alexandria, VA: ASCD.

Wiggins, G., & McTighe, J. (2012). *The Understanding by Design guide to advanced concepts in creating and reviewing units.* Alexandria, VA: ASCD.

Wilhelm, J. D. (2012). *Enriching comprehension with visualization strategies: Text elements and ideas to build comprehension, encourage reflective reading, and represent understanding* (Rev. ed.). New York: Scholastic.

Index

Note: Page numbers followed by *f* and *b* refer to figures and boxes respectively.

125

About the Authors

Jay McTighe brings a wealth of experience developed during a rich and varied career in education. At the school and district levels, he worked as a classroom teacher, resource specialist, and program coordinator. At the state level, Jay helped lead Maryland's standards-based reforms at the Maryland State Department of Education and led the development of the Instructional Framework, a multimedia database on teaching. He also served as director of the Maryland Assessment Consortium, a state collaboration of school districts working together to develop and share formative performance assessments.

Jay is an accomplished author, having coauthored 17 books, including the award-winning and best-selling *Understanding by Design* series with Grant Wiggins. His books have been translated into 14 languages. Jay has also written more than 36 articles and book chapters and been published in leading journals, including *Educational Leadership* and *Education Week*. He has an extensive background in professional development and is a regular speaker at national and international conferences and workshops. He has made presentations in 47 U.S. states, in 7 Canadian provinces, and internationally in 38 countries on six continents.

Harvey F. Silver, EdD, is the cofounder and president of Silver Strong & Associates and Thoughtful Education Press. A dynamic speaker and a leading expert on the use of practical, research-based techniques for improving classroom instruction, Harvey presents regularly at national and regional education conferences. He also works directly with schools, districts, and education organizations throughout the United States, conducting workshops on a wide range of topics, including student engagement, differentiated instruction, thoughtful assessment, instructional leadership, and strategic lesson/unit design.

Throughout his career, Harvey has worked to help teachers—and students—fulfill their potential. With the late Richard W. Strong, he developed The Thoughtful Classroom, a nationally renowned professional development initiative aimed at helping each and every student succeed. More recently, he collaborated with Matthew J. Perini to develop the Thoughtful Classroom Teacher Effectiveness Framework, a comprehensive system for observing, evaluating, and refining classroom practice that is being implemented in school districts across the country. Harvey is the author of a number of educational best-sellers, including ASCD's *The Core Six* and *The Strategic Teacher*. He is also the lead developer of the award-winning Tools for Today's Educators series of books, which provides teachers with easy-to-implement tools for enhancing teaching and learning.

Related ASCD Resources

At the time of publication, the following resources were available (ASCD stock numbers appear in parentheses).

Print Products

Compare & Contrast: Teaching Comparative Thinking to Strengthen Student Learning (A Strategic Teacher PLC Guide) by Harvey F. Silver (#110126)

Cultivating Curiosity in K–12 Classrooms: How to Promote and Sustain Deep Learning by Wendy L. Ostroff (#116001)

Designing Authentic Performance Tasks and Projects: Tools for Meaningful Learning and Assessment by Jay McTighe, Kristina J. Doubet, and Eric Carbaugh (#119021)

Ditch the Daily Lesson Plan: How do I plan for meaningful student learning? (ASCD Arias) by Michael Fisher (#SF116036)

Essential Questions: Opening Doors to Student Understanding by Jay McTighe and Grant Wiggins (#109004)

The i5 Approach: Lesson Planning That Teaches Thinking and Fosters Innovation by Jane E. Pollock and Susan Hensley (#117030)

Learning in the Making: How to Plan, Execute, and Assess Powerful Makerspace Lessons by Jackie Gerstein (#119025)

Reading for Meaning: How to Build Students' Comprehension, Reasoning, and Problem-Solving Skills (A Strategic Teacher PLC Guide) by Harvey F. Silver, Susan C. Morris, and Victor Klein (#110128)

The Relevant Classroom: 6 Steps to Foster Real-World Learning by Eric Hardie (#120003)

The Understanding by Design Guide to Creating High-Quality Units by Grant Wiggins and Jay McTighe (#109107)

What If? Building Students' Problem-Solving Skills Through Complex Challenges by Ronald Beghetto (#118009)

For up-to-date information about ASCD resources, go to www.ascd.org. You can search the complete archives of *Educational Leadership* at www.ascd.org/el.

DVDs

Core Six: Strategies for the Classroom DVD by Harvey Silver

Essential Questions DVD by Jay McTighe and Grant Wiggins (#614035)

ASCD myTeachSource®

Download resources from a professional learning platform with hundreds of research-based best practices and tools for your classroom at http://myteachsource.ascd.org/.

For more information, send an e-mail to member@ascd.org; call 1-800-933-2723 or 703-578-9600; send a fax to 703-575-5400; or write to Information Services, ASCD, 1703 N. Beauregard St., Alexandria, VA 22311-1714 USA.

WHOLE CHILD
TENETS

 1 **HEALTHY**
Each student enters school healthy and learns about and practices a healthy lifestyle.

2 **SAFE**
Each student learns in an environment that is physically and emotionally safe for students and adults.

 3 **ENGAGED**
Each student is actively engaged in learning and is connected to the school and broader community.

4 **SUPPORTED**
Each student has access to personalized learning and is supported by qualified, caring adults.

 5 **CHALLENGED**
Each student is challenged academically and prepared for success in college or further study and for employment and participation in a global environment.

ascd
whole child

The ASCD Whole Child approach is an effort to transition from a focus on narrowly defined academic achievement to one that promotes the long-term development and success of all children. Through this approach, ASCD supports educators, families, community members, and policymakers as they move from a vision about educating the whole child to sustainable, collaborative actions.

Teaching for Deeper Learning relates to the **engaged**, **supported**, and **challenged** tenets. *For more about the ASCD Whole Child approach, visit* **www.ascd.org/wholechild.**